A History of Methodism in Sutton-on-Hull

A review of over two hundred years of Village Methodism

Author and Publisher: J.D. Heald.
7 Wembly Park Avenue Hull.

All enquires to:
　　　　　Geoffrey Beecroft
　　　　　15 Cayton Road
　　　　　Hull HU8 0HD

Produced by: Burstwick Print & Publicity Services
Hull.
© 1993
ISBN 0 9521973 0 8

PREFACE AND ACKNOWLEDGEMENTS

In 1958, when we were discussing the approaching Church Centenary, the Rev. T.T. Rowe suggested that I go through the minute books and write a brief history of Sutton Methodism to be included in the Centenary Handbook. I agreed to do this, but unfortunately could not trace any of the minute books before Methodist Union in 1932. The result was a lot of time spent in the Reference Library, looking through old newspapers and any records that were available, and contacting local people who might be able to help.

The resulting account in the Centenary Programme of events was well received but also unlocked the secret of the lost records. I was walking in Church Street one day and met George Rodmell, an elderly member of a long established Sutton family who said, "I enjoyed that little bit of history in the Centenary Book, Mr Heald," to which I replied, "I had a difficult job finding the particulars because there were no minute books from past years." "No, there wouldn't be, would there." "Why, do you know anything about them?" "Yes, I was there." "What do you mean?" "Well, there had always been a lot of rivalry between Prims and Wesleyans so at Methodist Union, we gathered all those auld books together and bont 'em all i' school yard, to bury t' hatchet like and start a new life together."

Since 1990, I have occupied myself by recording a more detailed history, realising how unique is Sutton in that it is the oldest Methodist Society in Hull apart from Central Hall, with an unbroken record since the time of John Wesley. The present church premises are the oldest in Hull still in use for Methodist worship. Since 1800, 64 Methodist Churches or chapels have risen, flourished and faded or been destroyed by enemy action, while Sutton is still progressing and spreading the teaching of Jesus Christ to generation after generation.

Our members who became ordained have taken the Gospel throughout England, from Eastbourne in the south to the Shetland Isles in the north. It is a humbling thought that the seed planted in the Wheelwright's Cottage in 1775 must have affected the lives of many, many thousands and it is our hope and prayer that the growth may continue through succeeding centuries.

I am indebted to the following people or sources of information for help and encouragement, as without them, this History would have been impossible:-

"Sutton in Holderness" by Thos Blashill
The Hull Daily Mail for the use of photographs
The Rev. Frank Baker, B.A., B.D., Ph.D.
The Methodist Recorder
Bulmer's Directory
The Rev. A. Ernest Cook M.B.E.
The Rev. Leslie Reynolds, Late Rector of St. James
The Hull Chief Librarian (1959)
The Diocesan Register, York.
Mrs Merrill Rhodes
The Hull Times
The Rev. Brian Lewis B.A.

Sutton Methodist Church members, too numerous to name individually, whom I hope will accept this acknowledgement, and Mr Geoff Beecroft for his help in checking the script and typing it. Also Ron and David Forth for producing this book.

Sutton, March 1993

CONTENTS

Page
- 7. John Wesley.
- 8. The First Methodists in Hull.
- 9. The Sutton House Meetings and the First Chapel
- 13. The First Primitive Society and Chapel.
- 16. Wesleyan Expansion to Church Street.
- 24. 1897 Modernisation.
- 26. The Primitive Move to College Street.
- 30. Methodist Union.
- 37. Centenary Celebrations.
- 42. The New Hall.
- 55. Christian Stewardship.
- 58. Bransholme.
- 60. Three Men and One Woman.
- 64. The Sutton United Woman Meeting 1929
- 65. The Potterill Players.
- 68. The Groves Chapel.
- 71. Methodism in Wawne.
- 72. The Sutton Reading Room Society.
- 74. Methodist Churches and Chapels in Hull since 1744.

MINISTERS APPOINTED TO SUTTON METHODIST CHURCH

Prior to 1904, Sutton had no resident minister.

1904 Rev. G. Tulip Scott
1907 Rev. Robert J. Fenwick
1910 Rev. T. Allison Brown
1914 Rev. Frederick Sydney Bullough
1918 Rev. A.F. Hayden
1922 Rev. W.H. Harrison B.A.
1924 Rev. Reginald Cawthorne
1928 Rev. William S. Terry

Methodist Union
1933 Rev. John T. Ridley
1939 Rev. Frank Taylor
1943 Rev. Kenneth J. Towers
1947 Rev. Leslie J. M. Timmins
1951 Rev. John L. Warnes
1955 Rev. Trevor T. Rowe B.Sc., M.A., B.D.
1960 Rev. Kenneth R. Tucker B.A., B.D.
1966 Rev. David Coster
1972 Rev. Arnold S. Johnson B.D.
1979 Rev. John Girling
1987 Revs. David and Anita Green (U.S.A.)
1988 Rev. Michael P. Wilson B.Sc., M.A.

THE HISTORY OF METHODISM IN SUTTON-ON-HULL

John Wesley was born in 1703, the son of the Rector of Epworth Parish church, Samuel Wesley and his wife Susanna. She adored her pet son, Jackie, and her dream was that one day he would become a star preacher. Through the influence of a nobleman friend, he was given a free place as a boarder at Charterhouse School. After seven years at Charterhouse, he easily won a scholarship to Oxford University, and decided to become a clergyman. He was ordained deacon in 1725 and elected a Fellow of Lincoln College in 1726 and spent some time lecturing on Greek and Philosophy. In 1727, he helped his father for a time by acting as his curate and in 1728, he returned to Oxford to be ordained Priest. He had been joined some time previously by his brother Charles, a good looking poet and musician, and the two joined with friends to meet each morning for Bible Study and prayer, and soon became known as the Holy Club. In 1735, he and Charles went to Georgia in the U.S.A. as Missioners. They were an utter failure in the work and returned to England in 1737. During his sojourn in America, he became acquainted with a group of German Christians known as Moravians whose fundamental belief was that faith was a direct illumination from God, and that piety is little use without this saving grace. The brothers associated with a group of these Moravians in London, and on Whit Sunday in 1738, while recovering from an illness, Charles was filled with a feeling of God's presence, and when John came to see him, he was bubbling over with joy. Three days later on 24th May 1738 while attending a little meeting in Aldersgate Street, John's heart "was strangely warmed and he saw the light", and he felt that Christ had taken away his sin and he was "saved". He was a good preacher and longed to share his experience with others, but was condemned by his fellow clerics as a fanatic, and was not allowed to preach in their churches. His friend George Whitefield, an Anglican, was preaching in the open air at Bristol and was having to leave to go to America, and invited John to take his place. He soon found that he was preaching to crowds of more than a thousand, and built his first chapel there, naming it "The New Room" and it is still in use. He declared that "the world was his parish" and started his roving life as a preacher, travelling about 600,000 miles throughout the British Isles on horseback during his lifetime. He started "Societies" which were organised into "Circuits" and "Districts". He trained travelling preachers or "Ministers" who moved from circuit to circuit, and lay preachers to serve the local societies. He was ably supported by his brother Charles who used his gift of poetry and music to become one of the very greatest hymn writers.

As the Methodists spread, they became known as the "singing people" for they sang Charles Wesley's hymns at their meetings and in the open air. Previously there were no hymns as we know them, only dull metrical psalms. Charles took texts from the Bible as the basis for such hymns as "Come thou long expected Jesus", Joel 3-16, "Soldiers of Christ arise", 1 Tim 6, "Forth in Thy name, O Lord I go", Psalm 31, "Christ whose glory fills the skies", Luke 1 - 78.

Altogether he wrote about 6,000 hymns, the first collection in1737 in Georgia, followed by the "Morning Hymn Book" in 1741 priced at one shilling, and "Hymns and Spiritual Songs" in 1753.

The first Methodist Society was formed in London in 1739. Five years later, in 1744, Elizabeth Blow of Grimsby visited Mr and Mrs Medforth in Hull whose lives were changed and became the first Methodists in Hull. They started a society consisting of the Medforths, Mr Thompson, Mr Norman, Mrs Hird and three others, who met in a room in Back Ropery which is now Humber Street.

The early Methodists were viewed with a good deal of suspicion and dislike and on one occasion, our little group was besieged by a mob and kept in their meeting room till daybreak, when Mr Hird, a sergeant in the Town Guard came with his halberd to rescue them. Even so, the Society grew slowly, and in April 1752, John Wesley came to visit them.

He and his little group of followers led the way to Myton Carr outside the town walls where he was to preach. In his journal he says they were followed by a "large multitude, rich and poor, on horse and on foot and with several coaches". His sermon was well received, but even in those days, the town had its problems with hooligans, who gathered in force and broke up the meeting with shouting and throwing clods and stones. Wesley escaped with difficulty in a coach with eight others including a "Large Gentlewoman who sat in my lap" as he states in his diary. After this visit, the little meeting room was deserted for a better one in the Butchery, but this was soon exchanged for a larger and more distinctive one in Henry the Eight's

Tower, a relic of the old Suffolk Palace. Wesley came here in 1759, 1764 and 1766. Of the latter visit, he writes "The room was full at five in the morning". Converts were made, and little causes sprang up in the villages round about. In 1771, Hull became a Circuit Town and the Society purchased the Tower site, pulled the building down and built the Manor Alley Chapel, which bore the proud inscription, "This preaching house was built by the people called Methodists 1771, pro bono publico" (For the good of the people.)

Wesley described it as "Upon the whole, one of the prettiest preaching houses in England". After preaching there in 1774, he recorded, "The house would not contain the congregation. How is that town changed since I preached on the Carr".

It is now that we must leave Hull and turn our attention to Sutton.

From the early 13th Century, the religious life of Sutton was centred round the church of St James. The reformation period passed, and although it lost its College of Priests, St James still ministered alone to the spiritual needs of the village. However, with the 17th century came the rise of the Non-comformists, and in the middle of the century, several Quaker families were residents and indeed had their own burial ground.

At that time, it was necessary to register any house used for religious meetings, with the Diocesan Authorities. It is significant that in 1775, the year after John Wesley preached to packed congregations in Manor Alley, we find that the house of Robert Robinson, wheelwright, in the East End of Sutton, was registered for worship by Protestant Dissenters. The application was supported by John Bromly, Robert Turner and John Towers, apparently our first House Group of Methodists in Sutton. The D.I.Y. shop opposite the chapel, or rather the workshop behind, now a joiner's, was still producing wooden wheels before the second world war, and they were fitted with iron tyres across the road at Con. Calvert's blacksmith shop.

From the Parish register, we find Richard Robinson and Susannah Watson were married on 17th December, 1734, and Robert, son of Richard Robinson was baptised on 7th July, 1735. "Robert Robinson and Frances Usward, both of this parish married on 21st June, 1756." Thus we see that Robert married at the age of 21, and started the first House Meeting at the age of 40. Six years later, we find the entry, on "1st June, 1781, the house of Abraham Johnson, situate near Lowgate in Sutton near Hull, for Protestant Dissenters," and those associated were Willm Robinson, N. Ryley, F. Walker and Thos Plummer. I wonder if William Robinson was the son of Robert? Three years on, and the house of Nicholas Story and "adjoining buildings" were registered, by Wm. Ramsden, John Spence and S. Gartham. John Spence was a signatory for a "Methodist Preaching House" at Cottingham in 1783, and William Ramsden for Paull in 1797.

The cottage of Robert Robinsons, the Wheelwright, now Ayres DIY

In 1796, the barn of Mr Francis Harrison was registered and one of the signatories was Abraham Howden, a colourful Methodist Preacher. It is noteworthy that in the last two cases, the buildings of Nicholas Story were mentioned in 1784, and the barn of Francis Harrison in 1796.

"The Sunday Plan of The Methodist Preachers in the Hull Circuit 1808" shows that a regular Sunday Service was held at 6.0 p.m. in Sutton, and it appears the Society had outgrown house meetings and had now requisitioned barns for Sunday worship

By 1801, the population of Sutton had become 1,569 and the Methodist Cause was obviously growing stronger, with a need for separate Chapel premises. This is shown by the entry for 1809, "Registered December 19th, the said Chapel or Building for Protestant Dissenters." The signatories are called "Trustees of the Methodist Chapel" viz Sampson Middleton, Joseph Neal, and James Henwood were local preachers and the two latter preached at Sutton during 1808 (see plan). The situation of these premises is shown on the Ordnance Survey of 1855 to be that now occupied by the Reading Room on Church Street. The rear portion of the Reading Room is of different construction from the main building, and, with its round-headed windows, has every indication of being the old chapel (see reference to the Reading Room later in the History).We are enabled to get a glimpse of this early Chapel by means of the return made at the Religious Census of 1851. Lord Palmerston was responsible for securing an account of the Public Worship of England and Wales on Sunday, 30th March, 1851. It shows that at Sutton, the "Wesleyan Chapel" was a separate building used exclusively as a Place of Worship (except for the Sunday School). It contained 36 free sittings and 122 other sittings. (One of the main sources of income was from rented pews, but a number of free places were always left for the very poor and for visitors.) The attendance on 30th March was: Afternoon, 71, Evening, 100, Sunday School, 55, and the average attendance for the year was estimated at 65, 90 and 50 respectively. The steward who made the return was one George Cowl, a builder who was rather vague about the date of erection and stated that he thought it was about 1812. From the Diocesan Registry, it is obvious that he was three years out in his estimate.

During this period, a new popular, emotional and aggressive form of Methodism was spreading throughout the country. First known as

The SUNDAY PLAN of the *METHODIST PREACHERS* in the HULL CIRCUIT, 1808.

Preachers' Names	May					June					July					August					September					October				No.	Places of Meeting	Hours M	F	A	E
	1	8	15	22	29	5	12	19	26		3	10	17	24	31	7	14	21	28		4	11	18	25		2	9	16	23							
Joseph Bradford																														1	George Yard and Pottery	7	10¼	2	6
John Braithwaite	2	4		2	4	1	3		2		5	1	4	2		2		6			2	4	2			4	6	2		2	Scott-Street and Drypool		10½	3	6
James Needham	3		1	3	5	2	4		3		6	2	5	3		3														3	Scott-Street	10	2		6
Abraham E. Farrar	4	6	3			4	6		5			4	7	5		5														4	Thearne, or H. B. and Beverley	10	2		6
Humph. Stevenson	5	3	4	6	2	5			6		2	5	1	6		6														5	Seathorn, Roos, and Aldborough				6
Thomas Thompson																														6	Sunk, Keyingham, and Hollym				6
John Bruce	10	18		23	11		19		13		10		13																	7	Drypool				6
Thomas Cussons	8	15		11		23	9						14			10					20	11								8	Waterhouse-Lane				6
Thomas Williamson	14		13			10					11	14	21			14		23				20	16	2		14				9	Pottery and Groves		3	2	6
Joseph Neal	8	20		10			9	17				10	20	17		17					10		16			10				10	Stonferry and Drypool				6
Matthew Otley	13			8			8	18			15		14	21		15					11	5					21			11	Nestand				6
George Cookman																														12	Noabald and Walkington	10½	2	2	6
Thomas Slater	21	13		8		18		8			2	21																		13	Little Weighton and Cottingham				6
Thomas Reeves			9	22							14			15				20				19				8	18			14	Ellibughton and Welton		3	2	6
Richard Ellis	12			14	13		8				3		19	11		20	21				16			20			16			15	Antaby and Hessle				6
John Hill	23		11				12						3			13		15												16	Whorwmack, Elterby, & Coniston	10½	2	2	6
James Henwood	22		17	24		12		3			8					7	8	29				14	15				9	11		17	Skirlaugh and Sproatley				6
Sampson Middleton	8	15		12		11								7				10	22									15		18	Aldborough and Sproatley				6
Frederick Thwaites	17	9		11	21		18						21			20	13	19			22		4			19	15	17		19	Gumberthorn and Hedon		3	2	6
James Wheat, sen.	9		23	9	11	10		23				14	10	16				13				18								20	Paul and Marfleet				6
Henry Endson	7	9	21			9	22		10		17															9	10	21		21	Sutton				6
Thomas Livingstone	7								13		22	19	12													20	9	22		22	Burton and Preston				6
Robert Jackson	16		21	10		9	15			12		16				23					7			2					19	23	Cottingham				6
George Storr	14	10	16				21	13	9								12		18		22														
John Hobson			16		18									9			7	11				15		17				7	11						
John Mason	11	10	15	20		16		22	9		7		12				12					15		13		3									
Thomas Ryder				19				16					8			9		5	19			8		13		12									
William B. Briggs				14	13									16			20						20												
J. H.		20			15								10			10		9	21		11			8			10								

LOVE FEASTS.—GEORGE-YARD, *June 26th*, and *October 2d*.
BEVERLEY, *July 3d*, and *October 9th*.
COTTINGHAM, *May 15th*.
NEWBALD, *May 29th*.—Service to begin at One o'Clock.
SPROATLEY, Whit-Monday, *June 6th*.
ALDBOROUGH, *June 19th*.

SACRAMENTS at SCOTT-STREET, *June 5th*, *July 31st*, September 11th, and October 23d.
The Local Preachers will meet every Friday Evening, Half past Seven o'Clock in the New Vestry, in GEORGE-YARD.
The Quarterly Meeting for the Stewards, Leaders, and Travelling and Local Preachers, will be held in GEORGE-YARD Vestry, June 27th, and October 3d, at Ten o'Clock in the Morning.

Revivalists and later as Ranters, the members of the movement resisted the order and discipline of the Wesleyans, maintaining that evangelism was more important, and conducting open air and "Camp Meetings" in defiance of instructions to the contrary from the Wesleyan Conference. As a result, the leader of the movement, Hugh Bourne was expelled by the Wesleyans in 1808 and, with others, founded the "Primitive Methodist Connexion" in 1812. His followers at Sutton opened a Chapel in 1832 in Chamberlain Street at the corner of the passage from Church Street behind the Ship Inn. It cost £88/17/6 to build and had seating for 94 with an average attendance of 70. For the most part, the congregation was very poor and after sixteen years, the debt still remaining was £40. The majority would be farm workers, and it was in 1834 that the Tolpuddle Martyrs were transported to Australia for forming a trade union to protest about low wages.

The wages at the Martinmas Hirings in 1850 were as follows:

To "live in" or in "tied cottages":

Farm foreman	£25 per annum	9/8 per week
Waggoner	£18 per annum	6/10 per week
Plough lad	£14 per annum	5/5 per week
Woman	£15 per annum	5/9 per week
Secondary ditto	£11 per annum	4/3 per week
Young lasses	£1 per annum	4d per week

Married: tied cottage, rent free + free milk

At that time, a loaf of bread cost 8d so with a growing family to feed, a farm labourer would have little to spend on his Chapel.

In startling contrast, a craftsman such as a joiner or plumber received 4d per hour which would therefore yield £2, more or less, per week.

The list of Trustees for the next Wesleyan Chapel, which follows later shows some difference in the occupation of these Trustees.

Towards the middle of the century, the Primitive Methodist Connexion had no idea of the extent of the buildings in use, some owned by the local organisation, and some by private individuals so a questionnaire was sent out in 1848, and the following is a copy of the Sutton return:

CHAPEL SCHEDULE 1848

1. Report of the Sutton Chapel in the Hull East Circuit. What was the original cost of the Chapel? £88-17-9

2. Who was the superintendent when the Chapel was erected? Thos Holliday

3. What was the total debt on the Chapel when it was finished? £71-10-0

4. When was the Chapel built, and how many members were there in the Society at the place at that time? 1832 Do not know the number of members.

5. What was the number of inhabitants in the place or in the immediate neighbourhood? Cannot ascertain

6. What is the number of inhabitants at present? Do not know

7. How many members have you in society? 27 members.

8. How many persons is your chapel capable of accommodating with seats? 94

9. How many sittings have you in pews? 80

10. How many free sittings? 14

11. What number of persons attend on average your principal services on Sabbaths? 70

12. What is your average number of hearers on work days? 30

13. What is your present debt on the chapel or trust premises? £40

14. What is your estimate value of the chapel or Trust premises? £60

15. What amount of money has been expended on enlarging, altering or improving the Trust premises and what is the nature and extent of such enlargement etc.? Nothing

16. Is a Sabbath school taught on the Trust premises?	No
17. If so, what rent does the school committee pay the Trust yearly?	
18. Is the Title Deed connexial? If not, can a connexial Deed be made, and what would be the probable cost of such a Deed?	Yes
19. What was the amount of the Pew Rents for the last twelve months?	£7-12-6
20. How much is collected at your Chapel Anniversary?	£1-00-0
21. How much is collected annually towards defraying the expense of lighting and cleaning the Chapel?	£0-10-6
22. What was your total income and expenditure for the last year?	£9-03-0 Income
	£4-15-0 Expenditure.
23. If the property be leasehold and you pay a yearly ground rent, say to what amount, and how many years of the lease are unexpired?	Freehold

Signed on behalf of the Hull Quarterly Board, March 22nd, 1848.

    William Holiday (President)
    John Bywater (Secretary)

In 1852, two cottages and land at the corner of what was then Potters Lane, passed to a Mr Walter Wright from his mother, and on 1st June were sold to a Wesleyan Methodist Trust. The following notes are copied from the original deeds:-

"A Memorial of the written deed was registered at Beverley 23rd December 1829 at nine in the forenoon in Book E Page 253 and number 279.

Grace Frost, Widow of Thomas Frost, Charles Frost, eldest son and heir of Thomas Frost (both of Hull), and Robert Frost of Leeds. Sold for £125 to Mary Wright of Sutton:

All those two messuages or cottages situate and being in the Parish of Sutton aforesaid with the Garth, Gardens, Orchards and appurtenances thereunto belonging or therewith held and enjoyed, formerly in the occupation of Richard Clappison as Tenant or Farmer, thereof afterwards of Percival Frost, his undertenants or assigns, which said premises adjoin on or towards the north upon a lane leading from the Town Street aforesaid, southwards on or towards the east and upon herediments now or late of Thomas Ross on and towards the west and south, and contains by estimate 33 perches by the same more or less."

By an indenture dated 28th December 1852, the land passed to Walter Wright except for the cottage at the western side, which was to be in the possession of Mary Wright for the rest of her life, rent free. Mary Wright died 21st February, 1854.

"The parties listed in the second part being possessed of money intended to be laid out in the purchase of a piece of ground and hereditaments, and in the erecting and building thereon a Chapel or Place of Religious Worship, for the use of the people called Methodists, agreed with the said Walter Wright for the absolute purchase of the Messuages etc. for £160. A memorial was registered at Beverley the 16th November 1859 at nine in the forenoon in Book HY, page 191 and number 255 1st June 1859

Walter Wright of Hull, Tallow Chandler, sold to:-

William Hall	Builder
John Hall	Builder
Thomas Easingwood	Grocer
Richard Calvert Spicer	Merchant's clerk
Robert Stevenson	Farmer
George Cowl	Builder
Thomas Hall	Bricklayer
Luke Twidale	Farmer
William Sharp	Tailor
George Broombridge Barker	Joiner
John Hart	Farmer
William Hart	Shoemaker
Robert Coates	Gardener
Robert Londsborough	Farmer
Charles Curtis	Yeoman
Robert Carrick	Shoemaker
John Cowl	Joiner
William Dale	Miller

   All of the Parish of Sutton

Thomas North of Wawne	Farmer
Joseph Darby	Gentleman
David Moore	Merchant
William Carlin	Drysalter
James Robinson	Merchant
Jabez Bunting Dimbleby	Painter
Robert Waller	Builder

  All of Hull.

The Rev. Samuel Simpson, Superintendent Preacher of the Circuit.

All of those two messuages or cottages etc. and late in the occupancy of Mary Wright and one Esther Knowles, but now of David Wright and others. All which said hereditaments and premises adjoin upon the Town Street of Sutton aforesaid on or towards the north, upon a lane leading from the Town Street aforesaid, southwards on or towards the east and upon hereditaments now or later of Thomas Ross on or towards the west and south, 33 perches.

Modelled on the Trust Deed of Halifax 1832."

This transaction took place on 1st June 1859 and the following extract from the Hull Times of 25th June shows that the Foundation Stone Laying Ceremony took place barely three weeks later. It looks from this as if plans had been prepared, and a contract signed ready for a start as soon as the ink on the deed of sale was dry.
Hull Times 25th June 1859

NEW METHODIST CHAPEL Sutton

LAYING THE FOUNDATION STONE

On Thursday the service in connection with the laying of the foundation stone of a new Methodist Chapel, took place at Sutton. A great number of friends from Hull were in attendance, and the village assumed a very animated appearance.

The Wesleyan Methodist Society in this village has of late especially very much increased, and hence it is that the building of a larger chapel has become a work of necessity. A very eligible site has been obtained for the proposed building; and the society at Sutton has entered into the labour in a united and energetic spirit, and have already raised over £300 towards the project. The services of the day were commenced in the present chapel at half-past two o'clock by singing, reading the scriptures by the Rev. S. Simpson, and prayer by the Rev. J. McKenny; after which a procession was formed, comprising the school children, the ministers and trustees, and the friends. Arrived at the site of the proposed chapel, after further devotional exercises.

The Rev. S Simpson (superintendent of the East Circuit) made a few pointed remarks upon the subject of their assembling, and congratulated the society on having secured Mr Todd to lay the foundation stone of the new sanctuary, a person well-fitted for the work, both by his personal piety and devotion to the cause of Wesleyan Methodism. He then proceeded to state that a bottle would be deposited in the stone containing a document, of which the following is a copy:-

'The foundation stone of a new chapel (the old chapel, erected in 1808, having become too small), for the use of the Wesleyan Methodists of Sutton, in the Hull East Circuit, was laid by Mr W R Todd, on June 23rd 1859, in a catholic, not a sectarian, spirit - as the friends of all, the enemies of none - for the purpose of furnishing to the surrounding population additional accommodation for the worship of Almighty God; in the confident hope that, by the Divine blessing on the doctrines to be taught, the discipline to be established, the experience to be inculcated, and the morality to be enjoined therein, the glory of the Triune Jehovah in the salvation of multitudes of sinners, through faith in our Lord Jesus Christ, will be promoted; and with the earnest praye that all succeeding generations of Wesleyan Methodists may have gratefully and joyfully to adopt the dying words of their venerable founder the Rev. John Wesley, M.A. - "The best of all is, God is with us." The Rev. Wm. Burt, chairman of the district; the Rev. Saml. Simpson, the Rev. John McKenny, the Rev. Richd. Bell, ministers of the Hull East Circuit.'

Mr. J. Darby, of Hull, in the name of the trustees, then presented the trowel and mallet to Mr. Todd.

Mr Todd said - I deeply appreciate the honour the trustees have thus conferred upon me, and I will at once proceed at their request to lay the foundation stone of a new chapel, and may the God of Methodism bless the work of our hands. Mr Todd then, in a mason-like style, performed the preliminaries to the placing of the stone, which having been done it was safely deposited in its place.

The verse, commencing, 'Praise God from whom all blessings flow', having been sung, Mr Todd gave a few facts connected with the building of the present chapel, which he had collected from available documents. He said their present chapel was built in 1808, at which time the only Wesleyan chapel in Hull was that in Scott Street. The building cost £306.12s.4d; the subscriptions amounted to only £24.13s; and the collection at the opening was £10.9s.4d. By a strenuous effort made in Hull the sum of £54.6s.6d was collected, to be equally divided between Sutton chapel and Paull chapel. The total amount raised being £62.5s.7d. In 1809 and 1810 the income of the chapel was not sufficient to meet its outgoings, and an increase of debt took place to the amount of £26.13s.3d. In the present day they seemed to understand the art of giving better than their forefathers did; it might be that practice had made them to some extent perfect. But if they excelled the Methodists of old in giving, he feared they did not excel them in personal piety. It gave him great personal pleasure to be thus associated with Sutton, and he hoped that they would go on to prosper. He thought Sutton might in time become greatly extended - it might become an out-parish of Hull, and they might require a chapel as large as Kingston chapel. It probably would not take place in their day; he, however, wished them every prosperity with their projected building.

The Rev. Mr. Simpson then stated that the proposed chapel would be 43 feet by 40 feet on the outside walls; and 29 feet in height from the foundation. There would be attached to it ample provision for the children of the school; and it would seat about 500 persons; and he was happy to say that arrangements had been made for free sittings for about 140 poor persons. The style of the building would be Grecian. The cost was estimated at £1,017, towards which the friends at Sutton had promised £350; and they hoped to be able to raise another £317. He had great pleasure in calling upon the venerable chairman of the district to address them.

A plate celebrating the first Primitive Methodist Camp Meetingat Mow Cop in Derbyshire in 1807

The Rev. Wm. Burt spoke of the importance to the cause of God generally, to Weslyan Methodism in particular, and to Sutton especially, of the work they were then engaged in - the laying of the foundation stone of a house of God.

The Rev. McKenny addressed some very forceful remarks to the auditory, likening Methodism to a great factory, in which all were employed, when once the motive-power was given. In Methodism there was the pulpit, the Sunday-school, the class, the tract distribution, in which all might find occupation, while the motive-power was the Holy Ghost, which gave life to all their labours.

A collection was then made.

The Rev. R. Bell and the Rev. J. Sibree having each spoken a few words, the service was concluded by Mr. Simpson pronouncing the benediction.

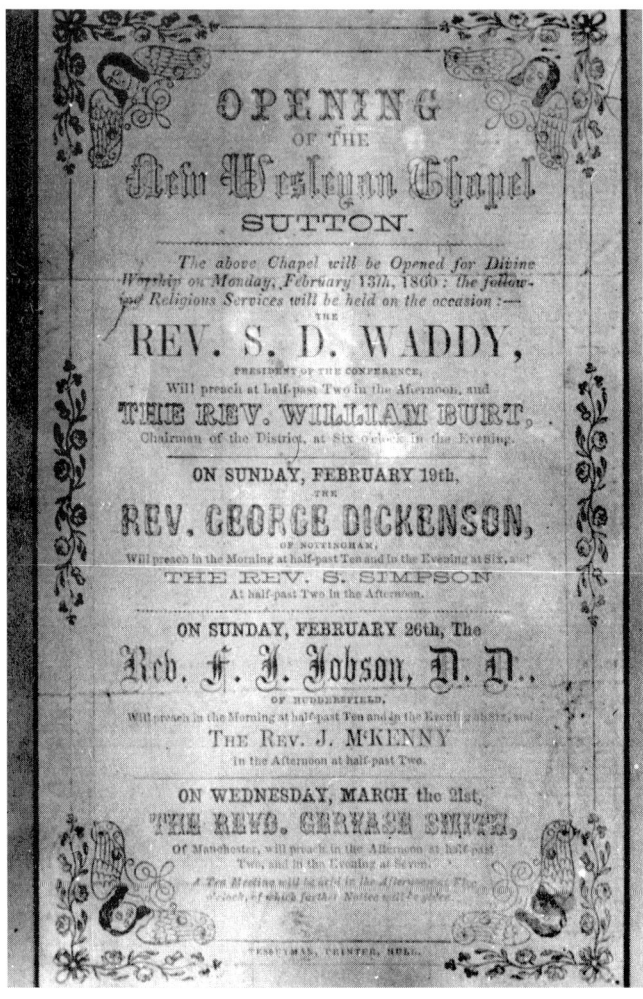

THE TEA MEETING

The vast concourse of people at the conclusion of the above service repaired to the field of Mr. Thompson, where a spacious marquee was erected, and provision made for an extensive tea-meeting. About 1,200 persons, including the school children, sat down to the repast, which was of a most excellent kind, and the gaily decorated tables and the good humour that prevailed made it an imposing sight.

After tea, the annual meeting of the British schools was held, R. Hardy, Esq. surgeon, of Hull, in the chair. The report having been read, the meeting was addressed by the Revs. R.A. Redford, J. Sibree, R. Bell, J. McKenny, J. Shannon, and J. Greenbury, and the proceedings were of the most interesting kind. There are at present on the books of the school 140 children, and the average attendance is 104. There have been 60 children admitted, and 66 left during the year.

The inscribed - stone on the gable end of the building shows the date as 1859, but in fact the opening did not take place until 13th of February 1860. The opener was the Rev. S.D. Waddy, President of the Conference, and the service was conducted by the Rev. W. Burt, the Chairman of the District

The Wesley Day school bell, 1860

In 1888, Forster and Andrews installed a pipe organ with one manual, 56 notes, eight stops, 480 pipes, a pedal board of 25 notes, and three pedals which could bring in a combination of stops. The organ could be blown either by hand or by foot and cost £130. The organ started life in the Wesleyan Chapel at Alford in Lincolnshire in 1857, and was replaced by a larger instrument in 1875, the original being returned to Forster and Andrews who overhauled it before selling it to Sutton.

Towards the end of the century, it was felt that the church was in need of modernising, and the old uncomfortable high-backed pews were removed and the present pitch-pine ones installed on the ground floor, and tip-up seats were fitted in the gallery. To our ideas, it is amusing to notice the wire frames underneath the seats, in which one's top hat could be placed out of the way.

The dado panelling on the ground floor, and also in the gallery, is formed of units which conform to the length of the pews and the width of the pew doors. Thus it appears that the old pews were not wasted, but utilised to line the lower part of the plasterwork of the walls.

At the same time in 1897, Mr Edward Good presented a new pulpit in memory of his wife and to celebrate Queen Victoria's Diamond Jubilee. The inscription on the pulpit reads:- "To the Glory of God, this rostrum was presented to Sutton Wesleyan Chapel by Edward Good. In sacred memory of his beloved wife Caroline Sarah who died March 7th 1896 and in commemoration of Her Majesty's Diamond Jubilee A.D. 1897"

It is rather sad to note that in the baptismal register, now unfortunately no longer available, the birth of a baby to Edward Good was recorded at this time and one can only come to the conclusion that this was a domestic tragedy, with the mother dying at child-birth.

Edward Good was a builder and contractor and a manufacturer of concrete reinforced cast lintels, window cills, etc. which would not be liable to rot like the previous timber ones. His works and "steam sawmill" were at 93 Barmston Street, Hull, and his residence, "Riseholm", Sutton. The present golf-house at the corner of East Carr Lane was named Riseholm, and I believe one of the houses on church Mount also bore that name, so it must have been one of these where he lived. For several years at the turn of the century, he was President of the Sutton-on-Hull Reading Room Association. It is worth noting that the pulpit receives special mention in the "Victoria Histories" as an extremely good example of the work of this period.

Popular education in this country really began with the schools set up by evangelical Christians towards the end of the 18th Century. They taught the 3 R's as a necessary preparation to study the Bible, and during the forty years after 1834, the Methodist British Schools Association built 850 schools. It is noteworthy that after the 1859 Stone-Laying, a meeting of the local "British Schools" committee was held, at which it was recorded that Sutton Wesleyan had 140 children on the roll, with an average attendance of 104, and adequate accommodation was being provided for a day school at the new premises. From this it appears that a school was already in being at the old Wawne Road Chapel. Bulmer, in his Directory records that there was a Wesleyan School at Sutton which received £27 per annum from the Chamberlain Charity for the remuneration of the Schoolmaster. Leonard Chamberlain was a Sutton landowner who died in 1716 and left property for the benefit of the poor in Sutton and Stoneferry. When the School Boards were set up in 1870, the voluntary schools received financial aid from public funds, and in 1892, the average daily attendance was 66. In 1902, the New Education Act abolished School Boards and replaced them with Local Education Authorities who assisted voluntary schools from the rates. The Potterill Lane school was closed in 1911 when the new Hull Education Committee school was opened at the corner of what is now Dunvegan Road.

The Wesley Day school , c 1895

During this period, the Primitives, not to be outdone, purchased a plot of land in College Street and erected a new building in 1855. I have been able to find little about the events leading to the opening of these premises. Fortunately, when I first took an interest in the subject in the 1950's, several of the older members of the church could actually remember events that took place seventy or more years earlier when they were small children. For instance, they remembered going to services in the old 1855 building after it was sold to the Salvation Army in 1876, because they were fascinated by the music of the band during the hymn singing. These premises were eventually demolished and Providence Cottages erected on the site. The building which is now the Masonic Hall was built in 1876 by voluntary labour from church members under the direction of Mr Fred Sewell, the founder of the present firm of F. Sewell and Son (Hull) Ltd., builders and contractors.

The workmen on the Primitive Methodist Chapel, 1876. The man at the back on the left is Fred Sewell

It is obvious that the Primitive membership now included a body of skilled craftsmen in addition to the original, mainly agricultural workers, with a consequent improvement to their finances. The venue for the traditional "Camp Meetings" was in "Mr Holmes' field", a piece of land in Lowgate to the left of what is now the "Lawns Club". The Society grew in strength and influence and in 1904, a Resident

Minister, the Rev G. Tulip Scott was appointed to take charge of the growing community. In 1907, the Rev Robert J. Fenwick replaced him, and the increased use of music led to a desire for a pipe organ. The Wesleyans had installed such an instrument in 1888, one with a single manual and restricted pedal board, so the Primitives now went one better. An organ builder, Mr Sherwood, lived in College Street, and he was commissioned to supply an organ with two manuals and full pedal board. This cost £250 but a grant of £125 was received from the Carnegie Trust.

For the next twenty five years, services more or less parallel with those of the Wesleyans were held, with Camp Meetings and Love Feasts taking place from time to time.

The American style Camp Meeting was introduced by Hugh Bourne at Mow Cop, a hill in Cheshire on 31st May, 1807. It could go on all day with a succession of speakers. The Love Feast dates from 1662 when the persecuted Covenanters were forced to hold services in secret wild places to avoid discovery. Later generations honoured these memories by a meeting at which favourite hymns were sung, and people stood up and spoke of their feelings and gave praise to the Lord. Baskets of bread and/or fruit cake were handed round, and water was drunk from a communal two-handled "Loving Cup". The Feast is carried on to this day at Alport Castles in Derbyshire.

The two pint cup used at the Love Feasts in Mr. Holmes' field

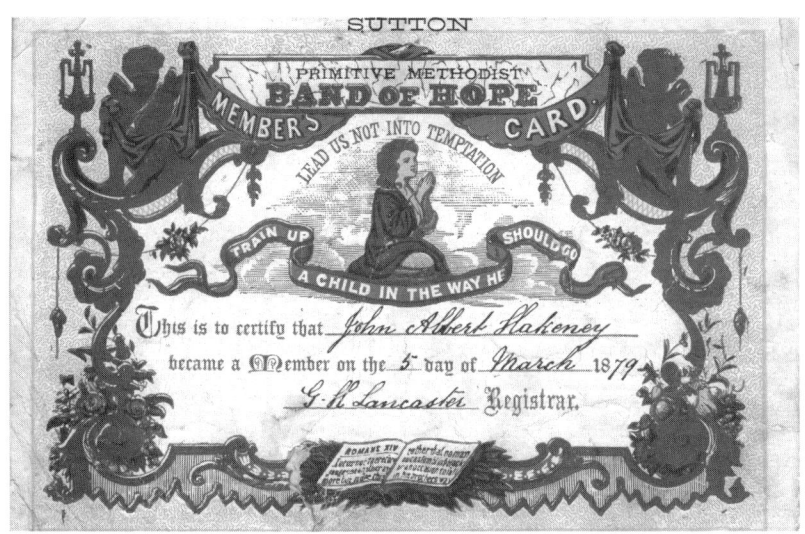

Above: Fred Sewell, organiser of the 1876 Primitive Methodist Chapel building, and Sunday School superintendent

Right: Mr. T.R. Pentith, Primitive Methodist Sunday School Superintendent, 1927

Above: Primitive Methodist Chapel, C. 1915-16

Right: Membership card from 1928

Below: Primitive Methodist Sunday School anniversary, 1906

Methodist Church, Sutton.

Celebration of the Amalgamation of the Two Methodist Churches in Sutton and

RE - OPENING SERVICES.

Thursday, December 15th, 1932 :

3-30 p.m. - RE-OPENING CEREMONY
Performed by Miss BARKER.

4-0 p.m. - SERMON
Preacher: Rev. REG. LOTEN (Bridlington)
Secretary Hull District.

5-30 p.m. - PUBLIC TEA.   Price - 1s.

6-30 p.m. - ORGAN RECITAL.   Mr. F. C. PAYNE.

7-30 p.m. - *Public Celebration Meeting*
Chairman - Mr. T. DODDS.
Speakers - Rev. REG. LOTEN.
Rev. W. HUNT FULLER.
Rev. T. PEARSON ELLIS.

Sunday, December 18th, 1932 :

10-30 a.m. - Preacher: Rev. WILLIAM S. TERRY.
6-30 p.m. -   ,,   Rev. W. HUNT FULLER.

At the close of the Evening Service the Sacrament of the Lord's Supper will be administered.

2-30 p.m. - *GIFT SUNDAY.*

RALLY OF SCHOLARS & PARENTS.

Children will bring Gifts of Toys for the Hull Methodist Mission (Queen's Hall).

Sister EDITH will speak and receive the Gifts.

Carols will be sung.

Monday, December 19th, at 7-30 p.m. :

Handel's "Messiah"

Soprano, LILIAN FINCHAM.   Tenor, CLEM HODGSON.
Contralto, GWEN BAGNALL.   Bass, ROBERT WISE.
At the Organ - HERBERT FULSTOW.
Conductor - ARTHUR ALDERSON.

Silver Collection.

METHODIST UNION

The greatest event in Methodism between the wars was its reunion. In 1907, three of the smallest Methodist Churches, the Methodist New Connexion, the Bible Christians and the United Methodist Free Church came together and founded the United Methodist Church. The idea of one Methodist Church came to birth between the wars, and was fostered by responsible leaders of the three great Methodist denominations, the Wesleyan Methodists, the United Methodists and the Primitive Methodist Churches. There was little theological difference amongst the Churches, though the Wesleyans tended to lay more stress on the Sacraments and had a "higher" conception of the ministry. Wesleyans tended to belong to the established middle classes and well-to-do tradesmen. Primitives with their origin deep in mining, heavy industries and agriculture, sprang mainly from the robuster working classes, though many were now emerging into the professions. The two smaller Churches were more eager than the largest one to consummate the union. They looked forward to belonging to a larger and more comprehensive communion than had previously been known. The Wesleyans were not so easily convinced of the practical advantages of the union, though their leaders were well aware of the need for unity and of the scandal of division. After the United and Primitive Conferences had voted decisively for the scheme, and the Ministerial and Lay section of the Wesleyan Conference had done the same, the final issue lay with the Pastoral Section of the Wesleyans. A seventy five per cent majority was required, and this was exactly what was obtained. The Uniting Conference was held in September 1932 and the new constitution followed traditional "Methodist" lines. The President of the Conference was always to be a Minister, with a Lay Vice-President.

The effect of the union on the higher reaches of the Church was immediate. Administrative departments and funds were unified, as was missionary activity. The theological colleges began to train a succession of ministers from all three traditions, and differences between them became irrelevant, and a new Hymn Book and Book of Offices were published. In Sutton, the two societies, Primitives and Wesleyans, had for some years worked together in friendly co-operation, on occasion holding joint services, so that the ground was already well prepared before Methodist Union took place. At this time, there was a healthy Primitive Methodist Society working in inadequate premises in College Street, whilst the Wesleyans, with better church buildings, were passing through a time of numerical and financial difficulty. Thus it was that on 2nd October 1931, the Sutton Methodist Union Committee under the leadership of the Revs W. Hunt Fuller, T. Pearson Ellis, and William S. Terry, decided unanimously:-

1. That the two societies should be amalgamated.
2. That the Wesleyan premises should be used.
3. That the United Society should join the ex P.M. Hull 3rd Circuit, as that circuit had already a resident minister in Sutton.

These recommendations were presented to the respective Leaders', Society, Trustees' and Quarterly Meetings, and Sutton must surely have been one of the first Societies to unite when Methodist Union became established at the 1932 Conference.

Representatives were elected from each former Society, and a loan of £500 was obtained, with which the Potterill Lane church was cleaned and decorated, and the organ from College Street dismantled and combined with the Wesleyan Forster and Andrews instrument to provide a wider range of sound. What had become the "Methodist Church" was re-opened on Thursday, 15th December 1932, by one of its oldest members, Miss Emily Barker, who was one of the last to be baptised in the original Wesleyan Chapel in 1859.

The preacher at the opening service was the Rev. Reginald A. Loten of Hornsea, and at 7.30 p.m., a Public Celebration Meeting took place, and a performance of "Messiah" on the 19th.

Prior to Union, the Trustees of the Wesleyan Chapel were as follows:

F.B. Rodmell	Deceased
W. Easingwold	Deceased
W.H. Hart	Desires to be discharged
G.W. Blakey	
P Slater	Deceased
A Carrick	Desires to be discharged
J.W. Jackson	Desires to be discharged
T.R. Ferens	Deceased
W.A. Gelder	Desires to be discharged
R. Marshall	Deceased
T.S. Taylor	Deceased
R.W. Scurr	Deceased
A. Wheelhouse	
William Simpson	Desires to be discharged

Victor Hart	Desires to be discharged
J.S. Wheelhouse	
H. Fellows	Desires to be discharged
T.P. Taylor	Deceased
T.Platt	Desires to be discharged
J.W. Wright	Deceased
W.H. Rodmell	Desires to be discharged
Percival Leech	Desires to be discharged
T.J. Ferens	Desires to be discharged
T. Dodds	Desires to be discharged
R.T. Godfrey	Desires to be discharged
W.H. Pridgeon	Desires to be discharged

The previouse Trust, (eleven of whom were members of the old Kingston, and Brunswick churches) was discharged and the following Trustees appointed:-

Wesleyan	George Westerdale Blakey	Wawne, joiner
Wesleyan	Albert Wheelhouse	Sutton, oil extractor
Wesleyan	John S. Wheelhouse	Hull, oil extractor
Wesleyan	Harold Copeland	Hull, lithographer
Wesleyan	John T. Gale	Hull, clerk
Wesleyan	William Henry Marrit	Wawne, farmer
Wesleyan	Clifford Marrit	Wawne, farmer
Wesleyan	Margaret Ellen Swan	Sutton, spinster
Wesleyan	Edith Nellie Wheelhouse	Sutton, married woman
Wesleyan	Emily Ann Barker	Spinster
Primitive	Herbert Sewell	Builder
Primitive	Thomas Robert Pentith	Sutton, cement executive
Primitive	George Henry Hodgson	Sutton, labourer
Primitive	Thomas Cross	Sutton, market gardener
Primitive	Clement Harold Hodgson	Sutton, joiner
Primitive	Joseph Charles Kirby	Sutton, blacksmith
Primitive	John William Mussett	Sutton, foreman cooper
Primitive	Terry John O'Brien	Sutton, oil manufacturer
Primitive	Hebe Hodge	Sutton, married woman
Primitive	William Barker	Sutton, gardener
Primitive	Ann S. Pentith	Sutton, married woman
Primitive	Richard Simpson	Sutton, school master
Primitive	Gertrude Longden	Sutton, widow
Primitive	Ida Mary Sewell	Sutton, married woman
Primitive	George Forth	Sutton, commercial stationer

The Rev. Hunt Fuller, Superintendent.

The memorial window at the back of the Church also dates from this period. The trustee, Mr T.J.J. O'Brien lived in Grove House, a large house in Tweendykes Road, His teenage son Terence sustained an accident to his leg which turned septic and caused his death. The inscription on the window reads:- "To the Glory of God and in memory of Terence O'Brien. Also to commemorate Methodist Union" It is the work of the late Samuel Harrison of Dock Street.

The College Street premises were now used by the Sunday School and Youth Club for meetings and concerts. The schoolroom was separated from the body of the chapel by a folding wooden screen, which, when folded back, made the schoolroom into a stage for the Sunday School concerts. With the outbreak of war and the appointment of the Rev Frank Taylor, the building now became used as a Hall, and amongst other duties, was used for the entertainment and recreation of the personnel from the Wawne Road R.A.F. camp and the anti-aircraft gun site. A canteen was run by volunteers, and Mr Taylor, who owned a cine projector and screen, obtained films and was able to arrange a fresh film show each week. To improve the view of the screen, the floor was raised by a team of chapel volunteers and airmen.

Mr Taylor finished his time at Sutton in 1943 and took away his cine apparatus. His replacement was the Rev. K.J. Towers, and as the war was ending, Mr Towers encouraged the Youth Club to produce plays such as "Farley Goes Out" and others. For this type of drama, a proper stage with "flats, backcloth and stage lighting" was needed. The Youth Club undertook the work and whilst it is onerous to name the many who took part in the construction, Ray Hodgson, Ron Forth, John Lowsley and the stage electrician Arthur Bellamy need special mention. Among the band of workers were Frank Godfrey, Syd Welbourne, and Harold Bowes about whom more will be told elsewhere.

The interior decoration had become very shabby so in February 1949, the Youth Club offered to undertake the decorating and also to improve the lighting. With paint obtained at cost price, and borrowed scaffolding, they carried out a quite professional operation. In this day, I think there would be howls of protest at the idea of the Youth Club attempting such possibly dangerous work.

For a number of years, in the 1940's and '50's, the Youth Club leaders included Stanley and Hilda Wheelhouse whose enthusiasm for work among the youth of the church was inspiring. A lot of the success of this period was due to their untiring devotion. They were largely responsible also for organising the canteen facilities for the members of H.M. forces.

For many years also, Stanley Wheelhouse acted as Welcoming Steward in the church porch for both morning and evening services. His cheerful greeting and firm handshake were the first introduction to the Sutton Methodist family for many newcomers to the village. Both he and his wife will be long remembered with affection.

In 1957, the Drama Group received notice that the College Street premises could no longer be used for public performances because of changes in the licensing regulations, and this led to greater need for a new hall. Efforts were made to sell the College Street premises and these succeeded in 1962 when the Brough Lodge of Freemasons became the new owners. All church activities were then transferred to the new Hall, to be described later.

The Potteril Players, "Man for the job".

To return to Potterill Lane, in 1947 the piped hot water heating system broke down, and Messrs King & Co said they could not even test the system before carrying out repairs. The heating system had been giving trouble for some time, so it was decided to ask the Hull Corporation Electricity Department to advise on a suitable method of heating. They contracted to do this for the Church, Primary Room and Vestry, by means of tubular heaters at a cost of £108-15-0 for reconditioned heaters and £84-15-6 for wiring and labour. This offer was accepted on 16th May, 1947. Miss Emily Barker gave £110 towards the cost of £193-10-6, and Mr Annison paid for the installation of the Deaf Aid apparatus.°

For several years, the question of a Manse at Sutton village had been under review. The original Primitive Methodist Manse had been at 32, College Street, and after Methodist Union, the Rev J.T. Ridley followed the Rev W.S. Terry into that house. In 1939, the Rev F. Taylor was installed into No 1000 Sutton Road which was apparently rented. When he left in 1943, the Rev. K.J. Towers was provided with the house No 57, Gillshill Road for a time, and then moved to "Katrine" at the Holderness Road end of Ings Road which was owned by the Circuit. But when the Rev J.L.M. Timmins came, in 1947, he was housed in an old three-storey house, one of three on Holderness Road, between Jalland Street and Village Road. The first tenants of these were Alfred Gelder, the architect, Joseph Rank, the miller, and between them, Thomas R. Ferens, at that time a clerk from Reckitt's, all of whom became of greatest service to Methodism during their lifetimes. The end house became Circuit property and the manse for Brunswick Church (now rebuilt as Holderness Road Church). They later re-housed their minister in the Garden Village. The Rev J.L. Warnes also worked from the Holderness Road house, and it was not until 1957, during the ministry of Rev T.T. Rowe that No 31, Highfield was purchased by the Circuit with financial aid from Sutton, and became the official Sutton Methodist Manse. This to us seems a ridiculous state of disorder, but we must remember that during the war, 86,715 houses in Hull had been damaged or destroyed, leaving an enormous housing problem in the post-war years.

In September 1959, 25 of the Trustees having died, or no longer wishing to belong, a new Trust was formed.

1960 CENTENARY CELEBRATIONS
6th March to 27th March.

At the Trustees meeting of 13th February, 1956, Mr Bellamy referred to the approaching centenary of the Church premises, and suggested that a committee should be formed to consider arrangements for a suitable celebration.

In September, 1958, it was decided to have the Church premises repainted inside and out by C. Pickering and Co., and the lighting re-wired and modernised by the "Atlas Electric Company". The organ was to be completely overhauled by Hall and Broadfield at a cost of £134 which was borne by Mrs H. Sewell. For the duration of the celebrations, the front of the church was to be flood-lit at night. During the renovation work, the Church was closed and the services were held in the Schoolroom. In the meantime, Mr Heald had researched the early history of the movement from the first Society in Hull in 1744 to modern times in Sutton. The Rev. W.H. Clarke, a Hull minister, had written the pageant, "Our Methodist Heritage" and with his permission, Mrs Edna 0. Pashby, the Church Drama producer, adapted it to include the growth of Methodism in Sutton. The programme featured the development of Methodism from that moment in Aldersgate Street in 1738 through the years, to Sutton, and finished with a 'Tableaux of World Methodism' which was the highlight of the Celebration. The cast numbered sixty one, the choir twenty six, and the organist was John M. Heald. A Centenary Exhibition was staged, with items from the Sutton of a hundred years ago, and events such as the following, filled a programme that lasted three weeks:-

Sunday, 6th March, 10.45 a.m. Rev F.W. Doar, 6.30 p.m. Rev T.T. Rowe, service for the reception of fourteen new members.
Monday, 7th. The Guides had an 'open night' when parents and friends were entertained.
Wednesday and Thursday, 9th and 10th. The "Centenary Pageant".
Sunday, 13th. 10.45 a.m. and 6.30 p.m., Rev Francis C. Godfrey, B.D., B.Sc., one of our own young men who had been ordained and was now Circuit Minister in the Burton-on-Trent circuit.
Sunday, 13th to Saturday, 19th. "Centenary Exhibition".
Monday, 14th. Concert by Hull Male Voice Choir.
Thursday, 17th. Centenary Rally with Prof. T.E. Jessop, Rev. Pratt

Green, and Rev. Douglas A. Griffiths.
Friday, 18th. Scouts 'Open Night'.
Saturday, 19th. Gift Day.
Sunday, 20th. 10.45 a.m. and 6.30 p.m., Rev. Leslie J.M. Timmins.
Monday 21st. Address by Mr Timmins chaired by Mr W.F. Wyatt, MSc
Thursday, 24th. Sunday School and Youth Club concert.
Sunday, 27th. 10.45 a.m., Rev. Trevor T. Rowe, B.Sc., M.A., B.D., 6.30 p.m., The President of the Conference, Rev. Eric W. Baker, M.A., D.D., Ph.D.

The Guides and Brownies, 1950

The Scouts, c 1950

Above: Guides and Brownies, 1960

Below: Part of the Centenary Pagent Cast, 1960

*** *** THE METHODIST CHURCH, SUTTON. *** ***

1860 -- 1960

WEDNESDAY, MARCH 9th, 1960.
THURSDAY, MARCH 10th, 1960.

at 7.30.p.m.

O U R M E T H O D I S T H E R I T A G E

A Pageant by The Rev. W.H. Clarke.
Adapted by Mrs. E.O. Pashby.

**** ******* ****

JOHN WESLEY played by LESLIE JACKSON.
STORYTELLER......GWYNETH BROWN, L.R.A.M.
SOLOIST..................RAYMOND KIRBY.
ORGANIST..................JOHN HEALD.
CHOIRMASTER.............JOHN W. PASHBY.
PRODUCER...............EDNA O. PASHBY.

**** ******* ****

"THE LORD IS MY STRENGTH AND MY SALVATION"

******

C A S T.

LADIES
Mrs. Scruton
Miss Cash
Mrs. Ducker
Mrs. Clark
Miss Crane
Mrs. Pashby
Mrs. Abbott
Mrs. Crane
Miss Snelling
Lois Clark
Miss Wiggins
Mrs. Pashby

GENTLEMEN
Mr. Jackson
Mr. Chicken
Mr. Abbott
Mr. Pashby
Mr. Kirby
Mr. Brewster
Mr. Lowsley
Mr. Townsley
Revd.T.T. Howe
Mr. Dalton
Edwin Bellamy
Robert Kirby,Jnr.
Brian Bell
Jimmy Bell
John Elliott
Robert Stevenson
Robin Beagle
Robert Robinson
Allan Bays

CHILDREN
Susan Branton
Margaret Toker
Susan Towse
Jill Beasley
Mary Greenwood
Lesley Warnes
Gillian Brock
Lynne Dent
Susan Brown
Geoffrey Branton
Philip Clark
Linda Murden
Richard Thompson
Susan Lowth
Norman Abbott
Melanie Cox
Susan Blood
Janet Kirby
Hilary Jibson
Aileen Cornell
Colin Snelling
Kay Malcolmson
Julia Bruin
Mary Wilson
Jennifer Cornell
Paul Scruton
Geoffrey Warn
Caroline Walton
Ann Barton
Pamela Grange
Linda Habbershaw

****

CHOIR

SOPRANO
Miss Burgess
Mrs. Jones
Mrs. Monkman
Miss Pashby
Miss Snelling
Mrs. Heald
Mrs. Bruin
Mrs. Fox
Helen Abbott
Margaret Wray
Winifred Townsley
Robina Moorhouse
Moira Kerr

BASS
Mr. Heald
Mr. Jones
Mr. Neale
Mr. Corrick
Mr. Rodmell

TENOR
Mr. Pratt
Mr. Fox

CONTRALTO
Margaret Jones
Margaret Pratt
Josephine Moorhouse
Mrs. Neale
Mrs. Williamson
Mrs. Kirby

***
***
***
***

DEAR FRIENDS,

Before, I begin to write about this new adventure, and it is an adventure to most of us in the Drama Group), I would like to thank, most sincerely, all who have helped to make it possible. I find it difficult to express how grateful I am.

Mrs. Pratt and Mrs. Abbott and the Women's Meeting, also the costumes; the choir, who have worked very hard, the children, bless them, they learned their parts without any bother to me; thank you mothers! and the cast, some of whom have never been on a platform before, but rallied round because I needed them. Thank you all.

We are grateful to the Revd. W.H. Clarke for his loan of the manuscript, adapted by me means that I added a little romance, and brought the story to Sutton, helped by Mr. D. Heald who readily supplied all the dates and history.

I come now to "OUR METHODIST HERITAGE" which is really a service of thanksgiving for our Centenary. There may be some who are inclined to think we have gone too far back, but we wanted to show how Methodism came to Sutton and that,of course, started with John Wesley.

At the end of the Tableaux, before the Benodiction, there will be one minute's silence————the silence of surrender; we would likeyou all to stand and speak the following GENERAL ACCEPTANCE, if you are willing to accept.

E. O. Pashby.

"I ACCEPT GOD'S FULL AND FREE FORGIVENESS, AND TAKE THE LORD CHRIST AS MY SAVIOUR.
BY GOD'S GRACE I OFFERR MYSELF TO DO WHATSOEVER MY LORD THE KING SHALL COMMAND.
I AM NO LONGER MY OWN BUT THINE. PUT ME TO WHAT THOU WILT, RANK ME WITH WHOM THOU WILT! PUT ME TO DOING! PUT ME TO SUFFERING! LET ME BE EMPLOYED FOR THEE OR LAID ASIDE FOR THEE! EXALTED FOR THEE OR BROUGHT LOW FOR THEE! LET ME BE FULL! LET ME BE EMPTY! LET ME HAVE ALL THINGS! LET ME HAVE NOTHING! I FREELY AND HEARTILY YIELD ALL THINGS TO THY PLEASURE AND DISPOSAL. AND NOW, OH GLORIOUS AND BLESSED GOD, FATHER, SON AND HOLY SPIRIT, THOU ART KINE AND I AM THINE, SO BE IT, AND THE COVENANT WHICH I HAVE MADE, LET IT BE RATIFIED IN HEAVEN."

OUR METHODIST HERITAGE

SCENE 1.	TABLEAUX PRE-MAY 24th, 1738.
SCENE 2.	JOHN WESLEY AND BETTY KIRKHAM.
SCENE 3.	THE SHIP SIMMONDS.
SOLO	'WHO IS THE STRANGER' RAYMOND KIRBY,
ANTHEM	TE DEUM CHOIR.
SCENE 4.	JOHN WESLEY'S CONVERSION.
SCENE 5.	FIELD MEETING.
SCENE 6.	ROBERT ROBINSON OF SUTTON.
SCENE 7.	MANOR ALLEY, HULL, 1774.
SCENE 8.	CHURCH STREET, SUTTON, 1775.
SCENE 9.	ROBINSON'S COTTAGE, SUTTON.
ANTHEM	'I WAS GLAD WHEN THEY SAID UNTO ME'. CHOIR.

TABLEAUX OF WORLD METHODISM AND FINAL CHALLENGE

SOLO	'RUGGED CROSS'. RAYMOND KIRBY.
VESPER	OH THOU THAT HEAREST PRAYER. CHOIR.

BENEDICTION.

***   ***   ***

A SILVER COLLECTION WILL BE TAKEN AFTER THE CHOIR HAVE SUNG THE ANTHEM "I WAS GLAD WHEN THEY SAID UNTO ME"

***   ***   ***

Tea and biscuits will be served in the schoolroom after the Pageant.....4d. each.

***   ***   ***

THE NEW HALL.

In November, 1948, the Trust decided that they should consider means of increasing the accommodation at Church Street and should explore the possibility of obtaining a site for new premises. A sub-committee was appointed consisting of Messrs Sewell, Musset, Morley, Bellamy, and Dalton to report later. In December, they suggested that F.Sewell and Son be asked to submit plans for the erection of a building in the school yard. In March, 1949, it was reported that the Town Planning Act would make a number of difficulties in carrying out this proposal, and Mr Sewell offered to make available a plot of land in Church Street to enable an entirely new building to be erected. The Trustees agreed unanimously to proceed with a scheme to erect such a building. It was also agreed that a building fund should be started and that an account be opened with the Hull Savings Bank to receive money for such a fund.

In May, 1951, the Rev L.J.M. Timmins felt that sufficient progress had been made with the Building Fund to approach the Chapel Department at Manchester to ask for approval of the scheme and to seek financial assistance. Mr Sewell had prepared a plan for a building to hold about 400 people at a cost of £5,100.

On 19th October, 1952, it was agreed that the College Street premises should be put up for sale. In 1953, W.B. Blanchard reported that planning restrictions allowed a very limited use of the building. From 1953 to 1957, all efforts to sell these premises failed because of Town Planning restrictions, and in January 1957, it was decided to place the sale in the hands of Messrs Sanderson and Co..

In 1958, a request was received from Southcoates Lane Methodists for the tip-up seats. This was agreed as long as they were responsible for dismantling and removal.

In May, 1956, sketch plans for the proposed hall were submitted by the architect, Mr Blanchard and were adopted as a basis on which to proceed. The death of Mr Sewell on 22nd July 1958 was a great loss to the Church. Not only was he a prime benefactor of the proposed hall, but a long standing support to all departments of the Society.

In June 1960, the Chapel Department agreed to the latest plans, and in October, the cottage, No 124, Church Street was purchased in order to rehouse the tenant of a cottage on the Hall building site.

Church Street 1958

Church Street 1960

In March, 1961, the tender of F. Sewell & Son of £14,000 plus architect's and surveyor's fees was accepted. In April, a final revised estimate of £15,500 to include heating, lighting, and furnishings was agreed. Building started in June and Mrs H. Sewell accepted the invitation to carry out the Stone-Laying Ceremony, which took place on 15th July, 1961. It was unfortunate that Herbert Sewell did not live to see the completion of the project in which he had played such a vital part. The Dedication Service was conducted by the Rev F. Pratt Green, Chairman of the District. This was followed by a tea and an Organ Recital by Mr W.E. Branton, A.R.C.O and an evening rally addressed by the Rev. W.H. Lake, Superintendent of the Hull Methodist Mission.

The Committee had been successful in raising a large part of the money required. The College Street building was sold to the 'Brough Masonic Lodge' for £2,000 the wartime reparations grant of, I think, £11,000 for the destroyed Groves Chapel was transferred to Sutton, a grant was received from the Chapel Department in Manchester, and the Sutton "Share Scheme" produced £1,543, leaving £1,615 still needed. As such a large sum had been received from the old "Groves Chapel" in Jennings Street, it was decided to preserve the memory of that Society by naming the large room at the back of the hall the "Groves Room" and a name plate was placed over the entrance. The opening of the New Hall took place on Saturday, 24th March 1962 by Mrs N.E. Wheelhouse, the oldest member. She was supported by the Rev W.O. Phillipson, General Secretary for Chapel Affairs, the Rev F.W. Doar the superintendent minister, the Architect Mr B.W. Blanchard and the Rev T.T. Rowe who addressed the Evening Rally, and preached morning and evening on the Sunday at the Service of Thanksgiving. The first programme in the New Hall was a play, "The First Easter" presented by the Potterill Players and produced by Edna 0. Pashby on the Thursday of Holy Week.

THE METHODIST CHURCH
SUTTON-ON-HULL

THE LAYING OF THE FOUNDATION STONE

OF THE

CHURCH HALL

Saturday, 15th July, 1961

3-0 p.m.

ORDER OF SERVICE

Opening devotions conducted by the Chairman of the District,
the Rev. F. PRATT GREEN

Except the Lord build the house, they labour in vain that build it. Our help is in the name of the Lord, who made heaven and earth. Blessed be the name of the Lord, from henceforth, even for ever.

Glory be to the Father, and to the Son, and to the Holy Spirit ; as it was in the beginning, is now, and ever shall be, world without end. Amen.

Hymn. (M.H.B. 703)

> City of God, how broad and far
> Outspread thy walls sublime !
> The true thy chartered freemen are,
> Of every age and clime.
>
> One holy Church, one army strong,
> One steadfast high intent,
> One working band, one harvest song,
> One King Omnipotent.
>
> How purely hath thy speech come down
> From man's primeval youth !
> How grandly hath thine empire grown
> Of freedom, love and truth !
>
> How gleam thy watch-fires through the night
> With never-fainting ray !
> How rise thy towers, serene and bright
> To meet the dawning day !
>
> In vain the surge's angry shock,
> In vain the drifting sands :
> Unharmed upon the eternal Rock
> The eternal City stands.

Prayer.

O Lord God, who art exalted above the heavens, and yet dost vouchsafe to dwell upon earth, and to visit with Thy presence those who call upon Thee ; look down in the abundance of Thy goodness upon us assembled in this place upon which we purpose to build for the service of Thy Church and the glory of Thy holy name.

Prevent us, O Lord, in all our doings with Thy most gracious favour, and further us with Thy continual help; that in all our works begun, continued, and ended in Thee, we may glorify Thy holy name, and finally by Thy mercy obtain everlasting life : through Jesus Christ our Lord. Amen.

The Lesson will be read by the Minister of the Church,

the Rev. KENNETH R. TUCKER.

1 Chronicles xxix, 10-18.

The Foundation Stone will be laid

by

Mrs. H. SEWELL

As the Foundation Stone is laid these words shall be used :—
"In the name of the Father and of the Son and of the Holy Spirit, I lay this Foundation Stone of a building to be erected here to the praise of Almighty God."

The Superintendent Minister, the Rev. F. W. DOAR, will conduct the Closing Devotions.

Prayer.

Almighty and everlasting God, who hast built the living temple of Thy Church upon the foundation of the apostles and prophets, Jesus Christ Himself being the chief corner-stone ; confirm and bless, we beseech Thee, that which we have now done in Thy name, and prosper the work to which we have set our hands. Remember, in Thy mercy, those who have planned and wrought, and offered of themselves and of their substance for the furthering of this work. Shield and defend those who shall labour with their hands upon the building, that they may receive no hurt ; and grant that this Church Hall now begun, may without hindrance and in due time stand complete in strength and beauty, a place fit for Thy dwelling ; through Jesus Christ our Lord, who liveth and reigneth and is worshipped and glorified with Thee, O Father, and the Holy Spirit, world without end. Amen.

Our Father, which art in heaven, Hallowed be Thy name. Thy will be done, on earth, as it is in heaven. Give us this day our daily bread. And forgive us our trespasses, as we forgive them that trespass against us. And lead us not into temptation ; but deliver us from evil. For Thine is the kingdom, the power, and the glory, for ever and ever. Amen.

Hymn. (M.H.B. 701). During the singing of this hymn the Offering will be taken.

1. The Church's one foundation
   Is Jesus Christ her Lord :
   She is His new creation
   By water and the word ;
   From heaven he came and sought her
   To be His holy bride ;
   With His own blood He bought her,
   And for her life He died.

2. Elect from every nation,
   Yet one o'er all the earth,
   Her charter of salvation
   One Lord, one faith, one birth.
   One holy name she blesses,
   Partakes one holy food,
   And to one hope she presses
   With every grace endued.

3. Mid toil and tribulation
   And tumult of her war,
   She waits the consummation
   Of peace for evermore,
   Till with the vision glorious
   Her longing eyes are blest,
   And the great Church victorious
   Shall be the Church at rest.

4. Yet she on earth hath union
   With God the Three in One,
   And mystic sweet communion
   With those whose rest is won.
   O happy ones and holy !
   Lord, give us grace that we,
   Like them, the meek and lowly,
   On high may dwell with Thee.

Offertory Prayer

Benediction

PROGRAMME OF EVENTS

3-0 p.m.	The Stonelaying Ceremony.
3-30 p.m.	SERVICE OF PRAISE in the Church. Conducted by the Rev. F. PRATT GREEN. Chairman of the York and Hull District.
4-45 p.m.	TEA in the Schoolroom.
6-15 p.m.	An ORGAN RECITAL in the Church by Mr. W. E. BRANTON, A.R.C.O., Organist of St. Michael's Parish Church.
6-45 p.m.	Community Hymn Singing.
7-0 p.m.	EVENING RALLY. Chairman: Mr. W. J. PURDON. Speaker: The Rev. W. H. LAKE, Superintendent of the Hull Methodist Mission.

TRIBUTE—

The Minister, the Trustees and Members of the Sutton Methodist Church wish to put on record their gratitude to the late Mr. Herbert Sewell, whose strong desire it was to give to the Church the site for the new Church Hall, and to his family who generously carried out his wishes.

APPEAL—

Estimated cost of the Church Hall	£15,500
Gifts and Promises (including gifts pledged through the Share Scheme)	£13,850
Still Needed	£1,650

Gifts will be gratefully received by:—
   The Rev. K. R. Tucker, 31, Highfield, Sutton-on-Hull.
               or
   Mr. A. S. Bellamy, 5, Guildford Avenue, Hull.

Left: Mrs. Sewell laying the Foundation Stone for the new Hall, 1961

Below: The New Hall Stonelaying, 15th July, 1961

The Rev Fred W. Doar, Brunswick, the Rev Walter Gill, Portobello, Mr B. Blanchard, Architect, the Rev Kenneth R. Tucker, Sutton, the Rev Fred Pratt Green, Chairman of the District, Conon Richardson, St. James, Sutton, and Mrs Sewell at the Stonelaying, 1961

THE METHODIST CHURCH

SUTTON-ON-HULL

THE OPENING AND DEDICATION

OF THE

CHURCH HALL

Saturday, 24th March, 1962

3-30 p.m.

THE OPENING CEREMONY AND SERVICE OF DEDICATION

Conducted by the Superintendent Minister,
the Rev. FREDERICK W. DOAR

The congregation will assemble in the Church Hall. The doors will be closed at 3-25 p.m. The Ministers, Officials and Guests will assemble in the Church Vestry at 3-15 p.m. and proceed at 3-30 to the Door of the Church Hall.

At the Door the Minister shall say:

Open to me the gates of righteousness: I will go into them, and I will praise the Lord.

The Architect, Mr. B. W. Blanchard, A.R.I.B.A., will present the keys to the Opener, Mrs. E. N. Wheelhouse, and shall say:

I present to you the keys of this building and pray you now to open it to the glory of God.

The Opener will Open the Door, and shall say:

In the name of the Father and of the Son and of the Holy Spirit I declare this Church Hall open to the glory of God.

The Processional Hymn (*unannounced*)—M.H.B. No. 64

The procession will move up the Hall and the members of it will take their places at the front.

Prayer

O God, Eternal and ever Blessed, who delightest in the assemblage of Thy people, receive us graciously as we come into Thy Presence, in the multitude of Thy mercies, and grant, we entreat Thee, that peace and prosperity may be found within these walls, that Thy glory may be the light thereof, and that we may be satisfied with the goodness of Thy house, through Jesus Christ our Lord. Amen.

The Lord's Prayer (*Minister and People*)

Hymn—M.H.B. No. 983

The Lessons will be read by the Minister of the Church,

the Rev. KENNETH R. TUCKER

1 Kings viii, 22-30

Matt. xviii, 1-10

THE ACT OF DEDICATION

The congregation being seated, the Minister shall say:

Beloved in the Lord, we rejoice that God has put it into the hearts of His people to build this Hall to the glory of His name. We now meet to dedicate it to His service. Let us, therefore, as we are assembled, solemnly dedicate it to its proper and sacred uses.

All standing, the Minister shall say (the people responding with the word 'Amen'):
> To the glory of God the Father, who has called us by His grace:
> And of His Son, who loved us and gave Himself for us:
> And of the Holy Spirit, who illumines and sanctifies us:
> We dedicate this Hall.
>> AMEN.

> For the worship of God in prayer and praise;
> For the extension of His Kingdom;
> For the promotion of His righteousness;
> We dedicate this Hall.
>> AMEN.

> For the teaching of the young;
> For guiding them in the way of faith;
> For leading them in the paths of righteousness;
> We dedicate this Hall.
>> AMEN.

> For the hallowing of family life;
> For the enlightening of those who seek the way;
> For the perfecting of the saints;
> We dedicate this Hall.
>> AMEN.

> In the unity of faith;
> In the bond of Christian brotherhood;
> In charity and goodwill to all;
> We dedicate this Hall.
>> AMEN.

> In gratitude for the labours of all the saints;
> In loving remembrance of those who have finished their course;
> In the hope of a blessed immortality through Jesus Christ our Lord;
> We dedicate this Hall.
>> AMEN.

Minister and People:
> We now, Thy people, compassed about with a great cloud of witnesses, grateful for our heritage, sensible of the sacrifice of our fathers in the faith, confessing that apart from us their work cannot be made perfect, do dedicate ourselves anew to the worship and service of Almighty God. Amen.

Minister:
> Accept, O Lord, this service at our hands, and bless it with such success as may most tend to Thy glory and the salvation of Thy people; Through Jesus Christ our Lord and Saviour. Amen.

Announcements and Offering

Hymn — M.H.B. No. 677

THE SERMON

will be preached by the General Secretary of the Department for Chapel Affairs, the Rev. W. OLIVER PHILLIPSON, M.A.

Hymn — M.H.B. No. 702

Benediction

PROGRAMME OF EVENTS

Saturday, 24th March

3-30 p.m. The Opening Ceremony and Service of Dedication
5-0 p.m.   Tea
7-0 p.m.   EVENING RALLY
           Chairman: Mr. ARTHUR CALEY
           Speakers: The Rev. W. OLIVER PHILLIPSON, M.A.
           The Rev. TREVOR T. ROWE, M.A., B.D., B.Sc.

Sunday, 25th March

SERVICES OF THANKSGIVING at 10-45 a.m. and 6-30 p.m.
Preacher: The Rev. TREVOR T. ROWE
The morning service will be a FAMILY SERVICE
There will be special music by the Choir

TRIBUTE—

The Trustees record their gratitude to all who have taken part in the work, and especially to the family of the late Mr. Herbert Sewell who gave the site, to the Architect, Mr. Bernard W. Blanchard, A.R.I.B.A., and his associates, and to the Contractors, Messrs. F. Sewell & Son Ltd., and all who have worked for them.

Grateful acknowledgement is also made to the Trustees of the Groves Methodist Mission who generously permitted their claim from the War Damage Commission to be transferred to Sutton, to the Secretaries of the Department for Chapel Affairs whose courtesy and generosity have meant so much, to the Joseph Rank Benevolent Trust for their financial help, to the members of the Sutton Methodist Church and other Churches of the Hull (East) Circuit for their loyal support, and to many generous people of Sutton who are not Methodists but whom we discover are our friends.

CHRISTIAN STEWARDSHIP CAMPAIGN

In the ten years from 1951 to 1960, the income and expense account showed a debit balance on seven occasions. This led to bank overdrafts and innumerable "efforts" to balance the books. In 1962, a committee was formed to overlook the whole of the Church Finances and to act in an advisory capacity. This committee suggested that we try a "Stewardship Scheme" with an expansion of the envelope system. It was realised that with the advent of the New Hall, the additional cost of maintenance would have to be met quickly. With Mr Heald as secretary, Messrs Forth and Dalton to organise canvassers and Mrs Branton as Hostesses Chairman, the campaign took place in October.

At the Leaders' Meeting of 15th February, 1963, it was reported that after fourteen weeks of the scheme operating, the average collection had more than doubled and by October, all outstanding debt on the New Hall had been paid.

In March, 1965, after three years of Christian Stewardship, the increase in costs gave rise once more to the question of financial security. It was agreed to hold another campaign similar to the one in 1962. This again yielded a satisfactory income, but the Rev Kenneth Tucker felt that the follow-up visitation had not been satisfactory, and that Pastoral Oversight was necessary. This was undertaken in 1966 when homes with a loose connection (i.e. Guides, Scouts, Youth Club, etc.) were contacted and a friendly reception resulted in a small but welcome addition to the congregation. The Rev David Coster, who took the place of Mr Tucker in September was able to announce at the November Leaders' Meeting that we had gained thirteen "New Members".

In July, 1968, finance was again a problem and it was decided to engage Mr F. Freeman, a professional organiser to conduct a major Stewardship Campaign in October. It was unfortunate that some members of the church objected to the "commercial" nature of a paid outsider conducting the Sutton Stewardship, and refused to take part.

The campaign was organised with attention to the smallest detail and lasted from 7th October to 1st November. To quote from a letter to all Members from Mr Coster, "In October, almost all the Church meetings are cancelled during the period of the Campaign. This is essential because it is necessary that every adult in the church can then hold himself-herself available to serve the Church in the Campaign."

Initially, the following teams were formed:- The Visiting Team, The Hostesses, The Arrangements Committee and the Finance Committee. Every home with any connection with the Church was visited, and the reason for the scheme explained, and the people invited to pledge a regular weekly sum to enable the Church to continue and expand its Christian Ministry. A supper was arranged at the Skyline Restaurant on Wednesday, 23rd October to which all were invited, the aims of the Church were explained, questions answered, and a report on the success of the Campaign given, with thanks expressed to all who had taken part. It was a financial success, the average weekly collections increasing from £30-18-3 to £60-16-5, which with Income Tax refunds on covenants took the annual income to £3,162.

In his summing up, Mr Freeman was very scathing at the attitude of certain Leaders and Trustees whose outlook was depressing and unco-operative, and failed the Church in this operation. However, the social nature of the scheme resulted in the formation of the following committees:-

1. Pastoral and Visitation
2. Finance and Policy
3. Youth and Christian Education
4. Social Services
5. Social

The "Class" system as we had known it ceased and the Class Leaders' duties were taken over by the Pastoral and Visitation Committee.

The success of the scheme may be judged, not only by the present state of the finances but also by the following organisations run by lay church members: The Cradle Roll, Junior Church, Junior Choir, Senior Choir, Youth Fellowship, Cub and Scout groups, Guides and two Brownie packs, Youth Club, Play School, Parents and Toddlers Group, Women's Fellowship, Wives and Friends Group, The Potterill Players, four House Groups, the World Mission Service, Home Missions Service and Women's Network.

In his summing up of the Stewardship campaign, the late Mr F Freeman said and I quote,

"The potential of this Church is tremendous if it is fully appreciated what lies ahead and the Church receives the right leadership. There is no doubt that this could become the first church in the East Hull Circuit.

While Sunday services are central to the life of the church, the corporate life includes purely social activities whose chief purpose is to form a meeting ground where people get to know one another, and where lasting friendships may be made."

I think that after twenty five years, Mr Freeman would have been happy to see the vibrant life of Sutton Methodist Church today.

Christmas 1962 saw the appearance of the first Newsletter. It was the brain child of the Rev K.R. Tucker and in its first editorial, he says, "I want you to know what is going on in the Church, and will announce services and meetings to keep you in touch. Secondly, this letter will give me another platform to communicate Christian truth. Twenty minutes and a sermon is done, another twenty minutes and it is forgotten. But the printed word is different and I hope it may survive a week or two in your home and may be picked up a few times and re-read." After the first issue, Miss Brenda Crane took over the editorial duties until July 1966 when she married and moved to Loftus with her husband. Her place was taken by Geoff Beecroft.

Practice time

In November 1964, the Leaders' Meeting under Rev. K.R. Tucker decided to hold a series of House Meetings involving a central theme of study. After almost thirty years, the "House Groups" are still a regular part of our Church life.

1967 saw early tenants at the Bransholme estate taking up residence and they were visited by the new minister, the Rev David Coster who had been requested by the Circuit to undertake pastoral oversight of the estate. In 1968, Methodist services were started in Dulverton School Hall.

1972 was the year that saw the Rev Arnold Johnson and his family arrive and also the appointment of a deaconess, Sister Marjorie Whitfield, to organise the new Society at Bransholme.

In 1970, the smelly toilet facilities in the school yard were typical of the "Rural Victoriana" of the previous century, and it was decided to erect a cloakroom with modern toilets in an extension at the back of the church. These alterations were completed in May 1971 by G. Clark and Sons at a cost of £1,385-10-0.

Radio Humberside broadcast a number of Sunday morning services from local churches in 1972-73, and on 11th January, 1973, it was the turn of Sutton Methodists. The Rev Arnold Johnson conducted the service with a full church and a very satisfactory recording resulted.

1975 saw the opening of the new Bransholme Methodist Church on Saturday, 22nd March. At 3.0 p.m., the Rev A.S. Johnson received the key from the architect and handed it to Mr P.H. Harrison, the senior Circuit Steward who unlocked the door. The Superintendent Minister entered and was met by the senior Society Steward, Mr H.V. Birkwood, and the Bransholme Methodists entered a new era, separated from Sutton, with a new identity of their own.

For some time, woodworm had been secretly attacking the Potterill Lane church and dry rot had been discovered in the roof. This led to a determined effort to eliminate both, at an estimated cost of £1,000. In June 1976, the Church was cleared of moveable furnishings and for several weeks, services were held in the Hall while workmen attacked the trouble with chemical sprays, etc.. When the smell had cleared, a group of volunteers cleared all the rubbish, and spring-cleaned the premises, ready for the Rev Paul Neal and his wife Mary from

Minnesota, USA, on an exchange of pulpits with Mr & Mrs Johnson.

August 1987 saw another transatlantic invasion with the arrival of the Revs Anita and David Green, a man and wife Methodist team from Houston, Texas. They were to stay with us for a year, and in that time they won their way into the hearts of the Sutton people and formed friendships that still continue though separated now by thousands of miles of ocean.

The current membership ticket

THREE MEN AND ONE WOMEN.

If a Methodist Youth club produces an Ordained Methodist Minister, it is cause for celebration. If it produces two, that is wonderful. But if it produces three contemporary ones, it must be almost unique. Yet that is what happened at Sutton in the 1950's. Thomas Charles Sydney (Syd) Welbourne, T.D., B.A., Francis C. (Frank) Godfrey, B.Sc., B.D. and Harold R. Bowes B.D., M.Th., all became Circuit ministers. It was during the ministry of Rev Kenneth J. Towers when they were all keen members of the Youth Club that they were affected by the sincerity of Mr Tower's teaching of the Gospel. This was followed by the powerful preaching of the Rev Leslie J.M. Timmins, and the atmosphere of the "Manse Fellowship Debates" led them to a sense of mission within the Church, and offering first as Local Preacher and then for the Ministry.

Frank and Harold were fellow students at Hull University College as it then was, and Syd was a member of the City Treasurer's staff at the Guildhall. Frank took a Diploma in Education and became a teacher at the Grammar School. Syd served his period of National Service in the 16/5th Lancers, and then Frank and he went to Headingley Ministerial Training college 1951-53, and, incidentally, Ken Tucker was in the same year with them. During Syd's first appointment at Pickering, he married Audrey Myers, an old friend from Youth Club days. He became a padre in the Territorial Army at Leeds for a number of years and took an active part in the annual camps, etc., an association which was to last all his days. Pickering was followed by Tadcaster, York and Hull West. He had a real concern for Youth Work in the Church and he was M.A.Y.C. District President for one year. This interest led him to apply for transfer to the Sector Ministry as he then would have greater scope for reaching young people who did not attend church. He trained for teaching at St John's College, York and taught first in Hull where he took the B.A. degree. His next post was head of Divinity at Millfield School, Glastonbury. Later, he came back to Hull and taught in the Prison Education Service, returning to Hull (East) Circuit as Minister, and Methodist Chaplain at Hull Prison. Unfortunately, he sustained a terminal illness and died shortly before he was due for retirement. For his work in the Territorial Army, he was awarded the T.D. (Territorial Decoration).

Frank Godfrey's first appointment was to Ashby-de-la-Zouche, followed by marriage to Wendy whom he had met while they were fellow students at University, and then six years at Burton-on-Trent. He became interested in work in new areas, and from Burton moved to Nottingham South Circuit which included an estate of 30,000 people, where the Clergy and Doctors had the only "private houses". He and Wendy took an active part in community work and counselling. The next move was to Crawley New Town, where again he concentrated on developing a relationship between church and neighbourhood. The following nine years were spent in the Redditch Circuit and included work in an Ecumenical Centre with the United Reform Church and the Anglicans in a church building which was the second floor of a shopping complex and was reached by lifts. Eastbourne Central was the final Circuit where he was Superintendent Minister, retiring to Gloucester to be within easy reach of his family.

Harold Bowes' National Service was in the R.A.F., and was followed by a period as Pastor at the Whitechapel Mission, London, where he met Maisie who was later to become his wife. In 1952, he was accepted for the Ministry and spent a year as Probationer at Saddleworth, followed by Ministerial Training at Headingley. He then married Maisie and they went to the Shetland Isles for five years. In 1960, he served in Gateshead, and this was followed in 1965 by a period at Lincoln North West. At both Gateshead and Lincoln, he spent a lot of energy on District Youth work. 1971 saw a transfer to Sheffield North, followed in 1978 by Sheffield Ecclesall where he served as Synod Secretary. In 1983, he went to Aberdeen and the North of Scotland Mission as Superintendent Minister. His final circuit was Worksop and Kiverton, again as Superintendent. On retiring in 1992, he settled in Barnsley.

The fourth member of our Ministerial team, Fiona A. Spandler was introduced to Sutton in 1976 and I think that as she is contemporary, it will be best for her to tell her own story:

" Perhaps I should begin with a little background information to my story.

"I was baptised as a child in the Church of England but due to circumstances, did not attend church or Sunday School.

"When I was 20 years of age and working at Kingston General Hospital as a Medical Laboratory Technician, a number of different experiences led me to a commitment to God. I began to look for a church in order to learn more about the Bible and the Christian Faith. A colleague at the lab. was a member of Sutton Methodist Church and invited me along. So in October 1976, I began worshipping at Sutton church and was immediately welcomed into the church and young people's fellowship. In June 1977, I was made a member of the Church, in Arnold Johnson's time as Minister, and if I remember rightly, it was also when the Methodist Conference was meeting in Hull.

"The call to be a local Preacher came one Sunday when the Rev Harold Anfield had been invited to lead the Services. I remember he said, "God is calling someone in this congregation to be a Local Preacher." I later found that the message had spoken to two of us that evening, as a few years later, Mike Winfield also became a Local Preacher.

"In November 1979, I went with others from our fellowship to the M.A.Y.C. District Members Weekend at Greengables in Scarborough. I should have realised that something was bound to happen on a weekend entitled, 'Dare to be Disciples'. The sessions were ably led by Judy Coleman (now Brown) who was later to be appointed as the Pastoral Assistant at our Bransholme Church. That Saturday afternoon was a cold and blustery one, and others chose to spend their free time down at the beach! I remained in my room by the window, thinking. Suddenly I glanced down across the road into a workshop which was very untidy with tools and wood shavings, lying just where the workers had left them. Typical I thought, 5.o'clock Friday and they've dropped everything to be off for the weekend. I turned back to my Bible and found it open at the point in the Gospel story where Jesus had left the Carpenters' shop at Nazareth and gone off to the River Jordan to meet John the Baptist and begin his heavenly Father's work. As I was thinking about these things, a voice spoke to me and said, "I want you to leave your work and serve me, not just part time as a Local Preacher, but full time as a Minister". I later described this as a numinous experience and for me a distinct call which I have needed to look back on and believe in, since the way into Ministry is not easy nor is it meant to be.

"Testing times were to come and I still had to finish my Local Preachers' training under the Rev John Chilton and then Rev Arthur Valle, who was a Supernumerary Minister in Beverley.

"I candidated for the Ministry in 1984 and remember Cyril Townsley giving an assessment of me on behalf of the Circuit, as one of the different hurdles that have to be jumped in the year long process. I was surprised, and truly it was unexpected to pass through each stage achieving unanimous support and finally being accepted for training at the Queens Ecumenical College, Birmingham in October 1985.

"The College trains Church of England and United Reform Church students as well as Methodists and there are strong links with the Catholic Seminary in Birmingham. Meg Woodlock Smith had left our Circuit three years before me; she had also trained at Queens.

In September 1988, I was stationed in the Hartlepool Circuit with pastoral responsibility for a church of 220 members and a joint Methodist/Anglican Church with 20 members. In June 1990, I was ordained during the Cardiff Conference in Caerphilly Church with others from my College.

This summer after five years in the Hartlepool Circuit, I will (subject to Conference approval) move on to Bromsgrove in the Birmingham District. I am glad to be able to contribute my small part to the history of Sutton Chapel and its Members. Also to express my appreciation and thanks to the loving supporting fellowship, without which I am certain I would not be in God's service today.

Chapel interior, showing the combined Forster and Andrews and Sherwood organ, and the 1897 rostrum, which receives special mention in the "Victoria County Histories".

THE SUTTON UNITED WOMEN'S MEETING 1929

The Sutton Methodist Women had forestalled the official Union, as, from the Minute Book for 1929, it is obvious that they met alternately in the Weslyan School Room and the P.M. Schoolroom. For example, the missionary meeting on 12th September 1930 was held at Potterill Lane, a Service of Song on the 12th June 1931 in the Chapel at Potterill Lane, a Service of Song in 1932 at College Street and also at Wawne. In March 1933, a joint meeting with the Wesley Men's Fireside for an evening of songs and recitations was held, with a programme of Community Singing. Finally, the "Guild Room" at Potterill Lane was the regular venue. Annual garden parties were organised to raise funds, and took place at "Red Roofs" by the kind invitation of Mrs Pentith, "Grove House" by Mrs O'Brien, and "Chestnut House", the home of Mrs Sewell.

In 1942, the "Women's Meeting Knitting Party", later known as the "Methodist Comforts Fund" was formed. Wool, clothing coupons and money were collected to send out regular parcels to Sutton young men in the armed forces.

After the war years, the Meeting gained renewed strength, and under the guidance of Mrs S. Wheelhouse, devoted a lot of time and money to "Women's Missionary Work."

The Meeting also held many "efforts" to provide money in support of such charities as The Prisoners' Aid Society, the British and Foreign Bible Society, the National Children's Homes, etc. Annual donations were also made to Trust funds.

After sixty four years, the United Meeting, now the Methodist Women's Fellowship meets weekly from September to June with an average attendance of twenty five to thirty. The programme includes Members' afternoons, Devotional Meetings, outside speakers, Musical afternoons, slide-shows, etc. with a very friendly atmosphere and chatter over refreshments.

THE POTTERILL PLAYERS

In the early fifties , during the ministry of the Rev. John L. Warnes, a group of teenagers with Jon Cliff as producer, staged one or two plays in the old College Street premises. In 1954, Mr Warnes asked the Trustees to allow Mrs Edna 0. Pashby to form a Drama Section to operate on church premises. Permission was received and the play, "The Feminine Touch" was produced, and in 1955, the "Drama Group" was formed with the following officers:-

President: `	the newly appointed Rev. T.T. Rowe
Treasurer:	Miss B. Burgess
Business Manager:	Mr A. Scruton
Producer:	Mrs E.O. Pashby
Stage Manager:	Mr A Liggins
Electrician:	Mr John Land
Publicity Secretary:	Mr J. Pashby

"A Quiet Weekend" was produced in 1956 by Mrs Pashby with the assistance of Mr Roland Walsh. Because of police and fire regulations, the next presentation, "Job for the Boy" could not be shown at College Street, and instead, the St James Parish Hall was used.

During succeeding years until the New Hall was opened in 1962, the venue for the programmes varied from the Potterill Schoolroom, the Brunswick Methodist Institue in Durham Street, and the Co-operative Hall, opposite the New Theatre in Kingston Square. The latter building started life in approximately 1790 as the Medical School from the Hull Royal Infirmary and the facade was in a similar style to the Prospect Street Hospital.

With the advent of the New Hall, a fresh era opened allowing the stage, lighting and scenery etc. to be under permanent control, with accommodation for changing, toilets, kitchen for refreshment preparation, and seating for 150. The initial presentation was "The First Easter", produced by Mrs Pashby on the Thursday of Holy Week, 1962.

It was in the following year, 1963, that with the recruitment of Doris Kirby as pianist, the first "Old Time Music Hall" took the audience by storm, and now, thirty years later, the programme still retains the old magic. The colourful costumes, the old-time dancing, and the popular songs dating back to the beginning of the century are a combination that appears to attract all age groups. The Sutton Methodist "Potterill Players" are faced each year with a request for assistance which is sometimes greater than they can meet, and some applications have to be postponed until the following year. After the usual four nights performances in the Hall, the Players go on a tour to places as far apart as Anlaby, Beverley, and Keyingham with a version of the evening programme. Their entertainment is eagerly awaited at Old People's Homes and Centres, Sheltered Dwellings, the Centres for the Hard of Hearing, the Blind Institute, and Mentally Handicapped, and it is a joy to hear old and disabled people joining in the choruses. They are also in demand for fund-raising efforts for quite a list of Methodist churches, Parent-Teacher organisations etc. Alan and Doreen Scruton must devote an awful lot of their spare time to the planning and production of these programmes, and it is impossible to estimate the number of people who in a year are entertained by this talented, musical and colourful group of players.

In addition to providing these programmes, the Players also help with the church finances. When working expenses, materials and copyright fees etc. have been paid, the remainder is donated to Church funds. The first occasion in 1955 yielded £7 but the latest in 1992 was more than 120 times that amount.

Each year in the Spring, the Hall is packed for three nights for the production of a Drama, Comedy, Mystery or Thriller as the Players demonstrate their versatility in a quite professional display of acting. Thus, after forty years, another tradition has been built up in the social activities of Sutton Methodist Church.

The Potterill Players, "Jazz", 1990

Above: The Potterill Players, "Continental", 1991

THE GROVES CHAPEL

In the Middle Ages, the River Hull was a fairly wide, sluggish, tidal river with a thin deposit of mud left behind at each high tide. The silt gradually built up on the banks until eventually it was reclaimed, leaving the centre kept open by fresh water from the Holderness drainage area. This reclaimed land was known as "The Growths" or, as it eventually became, "The Groves". Early maps show it occupied, first by timber yards, and then by a few small ship yards. In 1838, the Hull Flax and Cotton Mill Company was built here, and in 1845, the Kingston Cotton Mill Company. The adjoining land belonged to Mr Robert Jennings, who sold it as building land, hence the name Jennings Street. By this time the population was overflowing from the old town, and by 1840, a network of streets of small houses is shown on the town plan. In 1897, a Wesleyan School Chapel designed by Gelder and Kitchen was built, with seating for 600, sited at the corner of Jennings Street and Cleveland Street. This Chapel, "The Groves" was badly damaged in the air raids of the 15th-16th April, 1941 at 3.30 a.m. and was subsequently demolished.

As a result of this action, a sum of, I believe, about £11,000 "War Damage Reparations" was paid to the Methodist authorities to be held for the advancement of post-war Methodist activities in the Circuit. This sum was eventually paid to the Sutton Trustees to assist in the cost of the New Church Hall on Church Street. In order to commemorate this generous gift, the large room at the back of the Hall was given the name "Groves Room" and a suitable name plaque placed over the entrance.

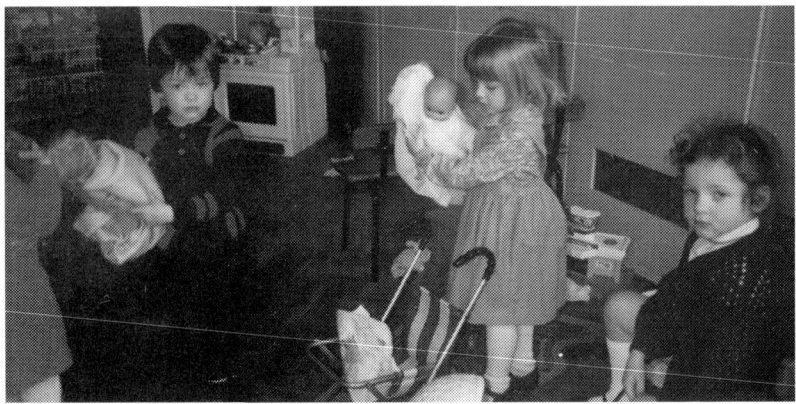

Above and Left: Sutton Playgroup, 1992

The Scouts' bed-push

Sutton Methodist Church Council
Back left to right: Mr Trevor Bettley, Mr Laurence Berry, Mr Phil Langdale,
Mr Allan Page, Mr Barry Renwick, Rev Mike Wilson, Mr Jim Maslen,
Mr Geoff Beecroft, Mr Alan Jarvis.
Centre: Mrs Sue Jacklin, Mrs Sue Langdale, Mrs Vera Jackets,
Mrs Doris Bolsover, Mr Syd Blackhurst, Mr Arther Kitching.
Front: Sister Agnes Notman, Mrs Barbara Lazenby, Mrs Margaret Bettley,
Mrs Barbara Berry, Mrs Elain Seymour, Mrs Dorothy Kitching,
Mrs Laurie Beecroft.
Nine other members of the Council were not available when the photograph was taken.

METHODISM IN WAWNE

The preaching of John Wesley does not appear to have made any impact on Wawne, and indeed, the Primitive Methodist Connexion Report of 1848 also makes no mention of any member there. It could well be that people from Wawne joined in with Methodist Worship in Sutton as one of the Sutton trustees was Thomas North of Wawne. However, in 1859, when the Potterill Lane Chapel was built in Sutton, a Primitive Chapel was started in Wawne and was opened on 2nd July 1860. It was built by George Calvert at a cost of between £100 and £150 and had seating for 70, and finance was raised by the opening date. This was due in part to the support of other Chapels in the district, by bazaars and gifts in kind, such as the 'One ton of artificial manure' which was sold by the Rev. C.G. Honor of Clowes Chapel at Beverley market and fetched £6-5-0. 68 out of the 70 seats were let at a rent of 9d per seat, and Wawne Chapel was free from the financial anxieties of many chapels.

In 1937, the Rev. J.T. Ridley, who had pastoral charge, planned to build a new chapel with a kitchen and lavatory, and in March, the necessary land was given by Mr J.F. Farnaby. Gelder and Kitchen were the architects, the builders were F. Sewell and Son, the cost was £800 and the new premises were opened just before the war in 1939. The old chapel was connected to the new one and became the schoolroom.

THE READING ROOM

The Trustees of the Methodist Chapel which was built in 1809, were Samson Middleton, Joseph Neal, James Henwood, James Shepherd Jnr, and John Richardson. In 1859-60, when this building had become too small, the Trustees, who negotiated its sale and financed the new building at Potterill Lane, included in their number John Hart, farmer, and William Hart, shoemaker.

In 1877, the Sutton on Hull Reading Room Society was established, and took over the old building which had become known as "Nancy Hart's Cottage". It is thus probable that the two Trustees had acquired the old premises and adapted them as a cottage for a female relative.

The Reading Room minutes of May 21st 1903 record that a sub-committee should be formed to draw up a reasonable plan for adding a Billiard Room to the present building, and to go into details of borrowing the required sum to build the room and acquire a full-sized table.

On 29th June, it was agreed to accept the tender of Mr F. Bilton of £112 for the building, and to obtain a loan of £200. The meeting of 18th November agreed to purchase a new table complete with balls, cues, and other fittings from E. Mawson of Leeds for the sum of £52-10-0, and on 11th December, 1903 the new room was officially opened, and Mr F.A. Scott and Mr H. Waterhouse played the first game.

By May 1907, it was felt that a bowling green would be a welcome addition, but it was not until February, 1909 that a lease was negotiated with the Ann Watson Charity for the necessary plot of land. The green was laid out by a Mr Brinkman for £38-10-0 and two sets of bowls were purchased for 15/6 per set, two jacks at 6d each, and two rubber mats for 4/- each. The official opening of the Green took place on 12th June 1909.

In 1913, a shooting range for air-rifles in the "Pavilion" was opened by Mr Stanley Wilson, and in 1914, the Reading Room and the Rifle Range were taken over by the military authority at a rent of £10 per month. The Trustees of the "Ladies College" in College Street offered the use of their schoolroom to the Reading Room Society free of charge for the duration of the war, and this was gratefully accepted.

A tennis court was laid out in 1917 and military officers were allowed to use it on two days per week at a charge of 3/- per day. This land was apparently rented, for in 1920, it was then purchased by the Society. By 1922, the following sections, each with a Secretary and Captain were taking part in local competitions:- Billiards Section, Bowling Section, Tennis Section, and Rifle Club, and a Ladies Room with facilities for whist.

It is thus obvious that the old Wesleyan Chapel had now become the centre for social life in the village.

APPENDIX

During the course of the research into the history of Sutton Methodist Church, data was collected concerning other Methodist Churches within the Hull area, data which is, in part, no longer available. For this reason, it is included here.

Methodist Churches in Hull

Opened	Name	Seating	Closure
Wesleyan			
1746	Back Ropery		To the Butchery
1752	The Butchery (Queen St)		To Manor House
1757	Manor House Tower		Rebuilt on site
1771	Manor Alley Chapel		To George Yard
1787	George Yard	1060	Closed 1905 for Queen's Hall
1804	Scott Street	530	Closed 1910 for King's Hall
1805	Raikes Street	250	Faded 1929
1814	Waltham Street	1500	Closed 1933, ownership retained premises used by Milday Mission
1818	English Street	?	Closed 1831
1818	Jennings Street	?	Closed 1834
1820	Lower Union Street	?	1928 became Jewish Mission
1820	Stoneferry Bethel	?	Closed 1892 for St John's
1826	Mason Street	?	Sold to Quakers 1851
1826	Lime Street	340	Closed 1841
1831	Alfred Street	?	Closed 1851
1833	Humber Street	800	Closed for Queen's Hall 1905

Year	Name	Capacity	Notes
1841	Kingston (Witham)	1200	Closed, war damage, 1941 Members transferred to Wesley
1842	Gt Thornton Street	1300	Burnt down 1907, rebuilt Thornton Hall, 1909. Bombed 1942
1858	Newland	200	Closed 1901 for new premises opposite
1865	Dairycoates (Carlton St)	300	Faded 1962
1866	Lee Smith Street	100	Faded 1910
1867	Beetonville	300	Faded 1954
1870	Oxford Street	300	Closed for King's Hall, 1910
1872	Trinity (Coltman St)	1250	Closed, war damage 1941
1873	Brunswick Tin Tabernacle		Rebuilt on site,
1877	Brunswick	800	Rebuilt on site again, 1962 as Holderness Road
1873	Marfleet, Hedon Rd	100	Sold 1910 for workshop on south side
1874	West Parade	400	Closed 1895
1876	Hamilton Place Mission		Moxon Street. Demolished 1930 for Ferensway
1876	Dansom Lane	340	Faded 1929, now Reckitt's Health Centre
1877	St George's Road	750	Amalgamated with Thornton Hall 1942, to become Thornton St George's. Demolished 1981
1878	Queen's Road	1120	Damaged by fire, closed 1967

Year	Name	Capacity	Notes
1882	Lower Union Street	100	Faded 1930
1883	Witham (Holderness court)	100	Faded 1906
1888	Fountain Road	400	Closed for King's Hall, 1910
1891	Anlaby Common	100	Closed for Anlaby Park 1914
1892	Barnsley St Mission	340	Closed war damage 1941
1892	Stoneferry St John's	240	Modernised 1962. Closed 1985
1895	Plane Street	800	Rebuilt 1910
1895	Argyl Street	1000	Closed 1959 to Spring Bank, sold to Anglican St. Stephen's 1972
1895	Providence Row	100	Faded 1937
1897	Jennings St. (Groves)	600	Closed, war damage 1941
1901	Newland	850	Rebuilt 1928
1905	Prince's Avenue	850	Part rebuilding 1993
1905	Queen's Hall	2000	Closed for Central Hall 1960
1908	Marfleet (Marfleet Ave)	200	Faded ?
1908	Wheeler Street	?	Faded 1911
1909	Thornton Hall	2000	Closed war damage 1942 amalgamated with St George's Road
1910	King's Hall	2000	Faded 1967
1913	Wesley	550	Now Kingston Wesley, amalgamated with Kingston 1941
1914	Anlaby Park	250	New building 1959
1930	Askew Avenue	?	Closed and rebuilt, 1985, due to settlement.

Methodist Union

1933	Derringham Bank	400	
1934	Endyke Lane	300	
1937	Preston Road	300	
1957	Bricknell Avenue		
1957	Greenwood Avenue (Clowes Memorial)		
1957	Nestor Grove (Bilton Grange)		
1959	Spring Bank		Faded. Sold to Anglican St Stephens, 1972
1960	Central Hall		
1962	Holderness Road		
1975	Bransholme		

Primitive Methodist

1819	Mill Street	750	Closed to Perth St 1908
1842	Wincolmlee		Closed 1872
1849	Great Thornton Street	625	Faded 1937
1851	Clowes (Jarratt St)	1415	Closed 1932 to Greenwood Ave
1864 1959	Jubilee (Spring Bank)	1030	New premises
1864	Bright Street	1100	Closed, war damage 1941 (Holderness Road)
1869	Bourne (Anlaby Road)	2000	Between Argyle St and Gladstone St Closed 1960, demolished 1964
1871	Stoneferry Emmanuel	210	Faded 1962
1872	Lincoln Street	950	Faded 1935
1873	Williamson Street	1300	Faded 1940
1873	Beecroft Street	?	Faded 1966
1877	Zion (Fountain Road)	800	Closed for Spring Bank 1959
1878	Ebenezer (Spring Bank)	1000	Faded 1946
1881	Hessle Road	1000	Closed to Elim 1934
1884	Hodgson Street	260	Faded 1940

1884	New George Street	100	Faded 1922
1888	Alexandra Street	80	Closed to Spring Bank, 1964
1889	Brighton Street	440	Faded 1960
1891	Edgar Street	200	Closed 1954
1894	Hedon Road	300	Closed 1941, war damage
1894	Lambert Street	850	
1897	Lockwood Street	100	Faded 1906
1889	Alexandra Road	?	Closed 1959
1901	Selby Street	400	
1902	Bethesda (Holderness Rd)	550	Closed 1962 to Holderness Road
1905	Hawthorne Avenue	500	War damaged, continued in schoolroom until 1955
1906	Portobello	610	
1908	Perth Street	350	Original building used as hall, new Church 1931.

Methodist New Connection

1799	Bethel (Charlotte St)	925	Closed, war damage 1941
1867	Osborne Street	680	Replaced by Boulevard 1907
1869	Stepney	100	Faded 1960
1907	Boulevard United Methodists	350	Faded 1970

Methodist Free Independent

1866	Campbell Street	560	Closed, war damage 1943
1902	Division Road	100	Closed 1907
1908	Pease Street	?	Faded 1910

Sutton is not included in these lists as it was outside the boundary until 1929.

ERRATUM

Page 38 Guides and Brownies 1960
Page 39 Guides and Brownies 1950

THE AUTHOR

Dennis Heald was born in East Hull, and as a boy, attended Southcoates Lane School. After leaving school, he served an indentured apprenticeship as a joiner. Attending evening classes at the old Hull Technical College, he obtained First Class Honours in City and Guilds examinations and, after a short time in industry, trained as a teacher. He taught for a while at Thrunscoe School at Cleethorpes and then in 1935 was appointed to Hall Road School in Hull, renamed Welton High School after the war, and became Head of the Department of Technical Studies, remaining there until his retirement in 1974.

His was a Weslyan family background, stretching back to the early days of Methodism. As a child, he attended the old Brunswick Chapel in Holderness Road, later becoming secretary of the Wesley Guild, and an officer in the church. It was here that he met his wife Alice, a pianist in the Sunday School and leading soprano in the church choir. After marriage, they came to live in the Sutton area, and joined the Methodists at Church Street. During his time at Sutton, he has at various times served as Sunday School teacher, Class Leader, Society Steward, Trustee, Chairman of the Stewardship Committee, Choir member, and member of the Potterill Players.

His son John became the Church Organist at the age of seventeen and continued until marrying the Brownie Leader, Robina Moorhouse and moving to Huddersfield. They now live in Lincolnshire and he is organist at the Grantham Central Methodist Church, continuing the family Methodist tradition.